CAMBRIDGE
Primary Mathematics

Learner's Book 5

Mary Wood & Emma Low

CAMBRIDGE
UNIVERSITY PRESS

University Printing House, Cambridge CB2 8BS, United Kingdom

One Liberty Plaza, 20th Floor, New York, NY 10006, USA

477 Williamstown Road, Port Melbourne, VIC 3207, Australia

314–321, 3rd Floor, Plot 3, Splendor Forum, Jasola District Centre, New Delhi – 110025, India

103 Penang Road, #05-06/07, Visioncrest Commercial, Singapore 238467

Cambridge University Press is part of the University of Cambridge.

It furthers the University's mission by disseminating knowledge in the pursuit of education, learning and research at the highest international levels of excellence.

www.cambridge.org
Information on this title: www.cambridge.org/9781108760034

© Cambridge University Press 2021

This publication is in copyright. Subject to statutory exception and to the provisions of relevant collective licensing agreements, no reproduction of any part may take place without the written permission of Cambridge University Press.

First published 2014
Second edition 2021

20 19 18 17 16 15 14 13 12 11

Printed in Malaysia by Vivar Printing

A catalogue record for this publication is available from the British Library

ISBN 978-1-108-76003-4 Paperback with Digital Access (1 Year)
ISBN 978-1-108-96418-0 Digital Learner's Book (1 Year)
ISBN 978-1-108-96419-7 Learner's Book eBook

Additional resources for this publication at www.cambridge.org/9781108760034

Projects and their accompanying teacher guidance have been written by the NRICH Team. NRICH is an innovative collaboration between the Faculties of Mathematics and Education at the University of Cambridge, which focuses on problem solving and on creating opportunities for students to learn mathematics through exploration and discussion: **nrich.maths.org.**

Cambridge University Press has no responsibility for the persistence or accuracy of URLs for external or third-party internet websites referred to in this publication, and does not guarantee that any content on such websites is, or will remain, accurate or appropriate. Information regarding prices, travel timetables, and other factual information given in this work is correct at the time of first printing but Cambridge University Press does not guarantee the accuracy of such information thereafter.

NOTICE TO TEACHERS IN THE UK

It is illegal to reproduce any part of this work in material form (including photocopying and electronic storage) except under the following circumstances:
(i) where you are abiding by a licence granted to your school or institution by the Copyright Licensing Agency;
(ii) where no such licence exists, or where you wish to exceed the terms of a licence, and you have gained the written permission of Cambridge University Press;
(iii) where you are allowed to reproduce without permission under the provisions of Chapter 3 of the Copyright, Designs and Patents Act 1988, which covers, for example, the reproduction of short passages within certain types of educational anthology and reproduction for the purposes of setting examination questions.

Cambridge International copyright material in this publication is reproduced under licence and remains the intellectual property of Cambridge Assessment.

Introduction

Welcome to Stage 5 of Cambridge Primary Mathematics. We hope this book will show you how interesting Mathematics can be and make you want to explore and investigate mathematical ideas.

Mathematics is everywhere. Developing our skills in mathematics makes us better problem-solvers through understanding how to reason, analyse and reflect. We use mathematics to understand money and complete practical tasks like cooking and decorating. It helps us to make good decisions in everyday life.

In this book you will work like a mathematician to find the answers to questions like these:

- What is a prime number and how do you know if a number is prime?
- How can you quickly find out if 642824 is divisible by 8?
- If three-quarters of a number is 24, what is the number?
- What time is it in Mumbai when it is 9 a.m. in Mexico City?
- What is a reflex angle?
- How do you draw a waffle diagram?
- How can a shape be translated?

Talk about the mathematics as you explore and learn. This helps you to reflect on what you did and refine the mathematical ideas to develop a more effective approach or solution.

You will be able to practise new skills, check how you are doing and also challenge yourself to find out more. You will be able to make connections between what seem to be different areas of mathematics.

We hope you enjoy thinking and working like a mathematician.

Mary Wood and Emma Low

Contents

Page	Unit	Maths strand
6	How to use this book	
8	Thinking and Working Mathematically	

10	1 The number system
	    1.1 Understanding place value
	    1.2 Rounding decimal numbers
		Number

20	Project 1: Decimal dice	

21	2 2D shape and pattern
	    2.1 Triangles
	    2.2 Symmetry
		Geometry and measure

35	3 Numbers and sequences
	    3.1 Counting and sequences
	    3.2 Square and triangular numbers
	    3.3 Prime and composite numbers
		Number

47	Project 2: Pattern prediction	
49	4 Averages 4.1 Mode and median	Statistics and probability

57	5 Addition and subtraction
	    5.1 Addition and subtraction including decimal numbers
	    5.2 Addition and subtraction of positive and negative numbers
		Number

67	6 3D shapes 6.1 Nets of cubes and drawing 3D shapes	Geometry and measure

74	7 Fractions, decimals and percentages
	    7.1 Understanding fractions
	    7.2 Percentages, decimals and fractions
	    7.3 Equivalence and comparison
		Number

87	Project 3: Puzzling percentages	

88	8 Probability
	    8.1 Likelihood
	    8.2 Experiments and simulations
		Statistics and probability

Contents

Page	Unit	Maths strand
101	9 Addition and subtraction of fractions 9.1 Addition and subtraction of fractions	Number
108	10 Angles 10.1 Angles	Geometry and measure

116	11 Multiplication and division
	    11.1 Multiplication
	    11.2 Division
	    11.3 Tests of divisibility
		Number

129	12 Data
	    12.1 Representing and interpreting data
	    12.2 Frequency diagrams and line graphs
		Statistics and probability

145	Project 4: Depicting data	
147	13 Ratio and proportion 13.1 Ratio and proportion	Number
154	14 Area and perimeter 14.1 Area and perimeter	Geometry and measure
164	Project 5: Picture frames	

166	15 Multiplying and dividing fractions and decimals
	    15.1 Multiplying and dividing fractions
	    15.2 Multiplying a decimal and a whole number
		Number

175	16 Time 16.1 Time intervals and time zones	Geometry and measure
184	Project 6: Time for bed	
185	17 Number and the laws of arithmetic 17.1 The laws of arithmetic	Number
192	18 Position and direction 18.1 Coordinates and translation	Geometry and measure
200	Glossary	
208	Acknowledgements	

How to use this book

In this book you will find lots of different features to help your learning:

Questions to find out what you know already.

> **Getting started**
>
> 1. Use digits to write these numbers.
>   a. Five thousand, two hundred and seventy-one.
>   b. One hundred and nine thousand and ninety.
> 2. What is the value of the digit 6 in these numbers?
>   a. 6703   b. 9060   c. 765 430
> 3. Copy and complete to decompose these numbers.
>   a. 805 469 = ☐ + 5000 + ☐ + ☐ + 9
>   b. 689 567 = 600 000 + ☐ + ☐ + 500 + ☐ + ☐
> 4. Zara scored 649 points in a computer game.
>   Which of the following is not a correct way to show her score?
>   a. 600 + 40 + 9   b. 600 + 49
>   c. 609 + 4   d. 609 + 40

What you will learn in the unit.

> **We are going to …**
> - estimate the size of an answer before calculating it
> - multiply whole numbers by 1-digit and 2-digit whole numbers.

Important words that you will use.

> frequency
> diagram
> line graph

Step-by-step examples showing a way to solve a problem.

> **Worked example 3**
>
> Write a different prime number in each box to make this calculation correct.
>
> ☐ + ☐ + ☐ = 10
>
> The prime numbers are: | Start by writing a list of prime numbers.
> 2, 3, 5, 7, … | Test different numbers to work out which
> [2] + [3] + [5] = 10 | ones make the calculation correct.
> | When you test numbers like this you are **specialising**.

There are often many different ways to solve a problem.

These questions will help you develop your skills of thinking and working mathematically.

> 5. Sofia is calculating 299 × 60.
>   She estimates that the answer is 180 000.
>   Has she made a good estimate?
>   Explain your answer.

6

How to use this book

An investigation to carry out with a partner or in groups. Where this icon appears, the activity will help develop your skills of thinking and working mathematically.

> **Think like a mathematician**
>
> You need four cards.
>
> [3] [5] [4] [6]
>
> Arrange the cards as a multiplication calculation. 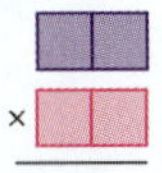
> Investigate different answers. Try to find as many as you can and then find the largest and smallest answers.
> You will show you are **specialising** when you find solutions to the problem.

Questions to help you think about how you learn.

> Think about the questions in this exercise. Which question was the most difficult? If you were asked to do a similar question, what would you do differently?

This is what you have learned in the unit.

> **Look what I can do!**
>
> ☐ I can estimate the size of an answer before calculating it.
> ☐ I can divide whole numbers by 1-digit whole numbers.

Questions that cover what you have learned in the unit.

> **Check your progress**
>
> 1. Calculate.
>   a 408 × 7   b 46 × 24   c 504 ÷ 9
> 2. Calculate, writing the remainder as a fraction.
>   a 98 ÷ 5   b 86 ÷ 3   c 89 ÷ 7
> 3. Copy the sorting diagram. Write these numbers in the correct place on the diagram.
>   23 456   51 466   62 848   76 343   97 631

 > Project 2

At the end of several units, there is a project for you to carry out using what you have learned. You might make something or solve a problem.

Projects and their accompanying teacher guidance have been written by the NRICH Team. NRICH is an innovative collaboration between the Faculties of Mathematics and Education at the University of Cambridge, which focuses on problem solving and on creating opportunities for students to learn mathematics through exploration and discussion: nrich.maths.org.

> **Pattern prediction**
>
> Marcus and Zara were asked to draw this matchstick pattern:
>
> Marcus drew this first:
>
> Then he added more to make this:
>
> Then this:
>
> Then finally:
>
> Can you describe how Marcus drew the pattern?
> How many triangles did he draw?
> How many matchsticks did he use in the finished picture?

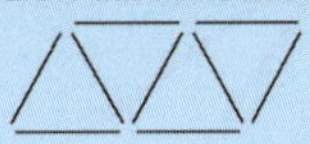

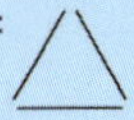

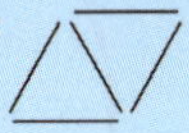

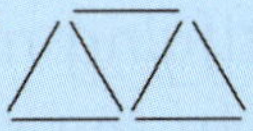

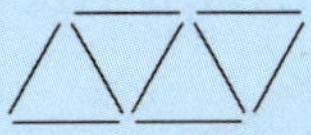

Thinking and Working Mathematically

There are some important skills that you will develop as you learn mathematics.

Specialising is when I choose an example and check to see if it satisfies or does not satisfy specific mathematical criteria.

Characterising is when I identify and describe the mathematical properties of an object.

Generalising is when I recognise an underlying pattern by identifying many examples that satisfy the same mathematical criteria.

Classifying is when I organise objects into groups according to their mathematical properties.

Thinking and Working Mathematically

Critiquing is when I compare and evaluate mathematical ideas, representations or solutions to identify advantages and disadvantages.

Improving is when I refine mathematical ideas or representations to develop a more effective approach or solution.

Conjecturing is when I form mathematical questions or ideas.

Convincing is when I present evidence to justify or challenge a mathematical idea or solution.

1 The number system

Getting started

1. Use digits to write these numbers.
   - a Five thousand, two hundred and seventy-one.
   - b One hundred and nine thousand and ninety.

2. What is the value of the digit 6 in these numbers?
   - a 6703
   - b 9060
   - c 765 430

3. Copy and complete to decompose these numbers.
   - a 805 469 = ☐ + 5000 + ☐ + ☐ + 9
   - b 689 567 = 600 000 + ☐ + ☐ + 500 + ☐ + ☐

4. Zara scored 649 points in a computer game.
   Which of the following is not a correct way to show her score?
   - A 600 + 40 + 9
   - B 600 + 49
   - C 609 + 4
   - D 609 + 40

5. Which of these numbers is 100 times larger than three hundred and thirty-three?
   - A 333
   - B 3330
   - C 33 300
   - D 333 000

6. Write the missing numbers.
   - a ☐ ÷ 10 = 64
   - b 509 × ☐ = 5090
   - c ☐ × 100 = 8000
   - d 4400 ÷ ☐ = 44

1 The number system

Place value is important because it helps you understand the meaning of a number. You need place value to understand the order of numbers. If someone offers you 30 dollars or 300 dollars, you need to know that 300 is more than 30.

When you go shopping you will see lots of price labels.

What do these labels have in common?

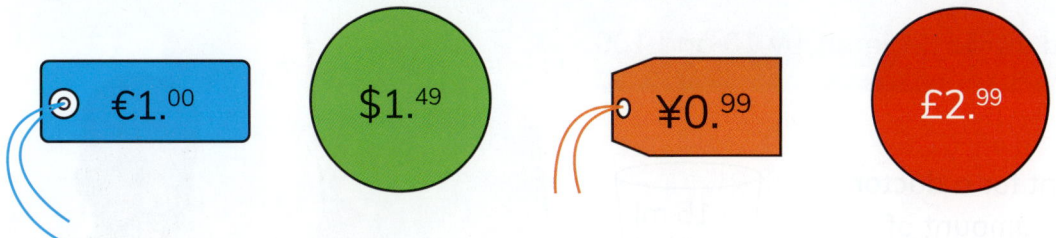

In this unit you will learn more about decimal numbers. Look at the examples in these pictures and talk with your partner about where you have seen decimal numbers.

1 The number system

> 1.1 Understanding place value

We are going to ...

- explain the value of a digit in a decimal number (tenths and hundredths)
- multiply and divide whole numbers by 1000
- multiply and divide decimals by 10 and 100.

It is very important for a doctor to give the correct amount of medicine. A dose of 10 ml is ten times greater than a dose of 1 ml and ten times smaller than a dose of 100 ml.

> compose   decimal   decimal place
> decimal point   decompose   hundredth
> place value   tenth

The value of a digit depends on its position in the number. Think about what the digit 5 is worth in these numbers.

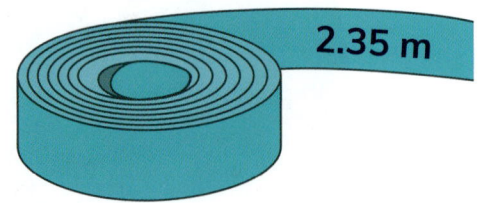

2.35 m

25 cents

1.1 Understanding place value

> **Worked example 1**
>
> Write this number in words and digits.
>
> 10 000 + 2000 + 300 + 40 + 5 + 0.6 + 0.07

Answer:

12 345.67

Twelve thousand, three hundred and forty-five point six seven.

Use a place value grid to help you.

Tip

Remember to write the decimal part of the number as 'six seven' and not as 'sixty-seven'.

10 000s	1000s	100s	10s	1s	$\frac{1}{10}$s	$\frac{1}{100}$s
1	2	3	4	5	6	7

ten thousands ↓ ... tenths ↓   hundredths ↓

Exercise 1.1

1. Write these numbers in digits.
   a. One thousand and one point zero one
   b. Five hundred thousand and five point nine
   c. Four hundred and three thousand, and thirty-four point six six

2. Write these numbers in words.
   a. 345.09
   b. 5378.12
   c. 158 035.4
   d. 3030.03

3. What is the value of the digit 7 in these numbers?
   a. 6703.46
   b. 70 213.8
   c. 606 456.7
   d. 234 560.07

1 The number system

4 Write these numbers in words and digits.

   a 200 000 + 6000 + 300 + 2 + 0.1

   b 900 000 + 90 000 + 900 + 9 + 0.9

   c 100 000 + 20 000 + 5000 + 600 + 20 + 5 + 0.4 + 0.03

   Swap books with your partner and check their answers.

5 Write the missing numbers.

   a 358 × 100 = ☐   b 2700 ÷ ☐ = 27

   c 5600 ÷ 1000 = ☐   d 456 × 1000 = ☐

6 Sofia multiplies a number by 10, then again by 10 and then again by 10.

   Her answer is 20 000.

   What number did she start with?

7 Write the missing numbers.

   a 3.45 × 100 = ☐   b 16.8 ÷ 10 = ☐

   c 6.5 × 10 = ☐

  8 Find and correct the mistakes in this diagram.

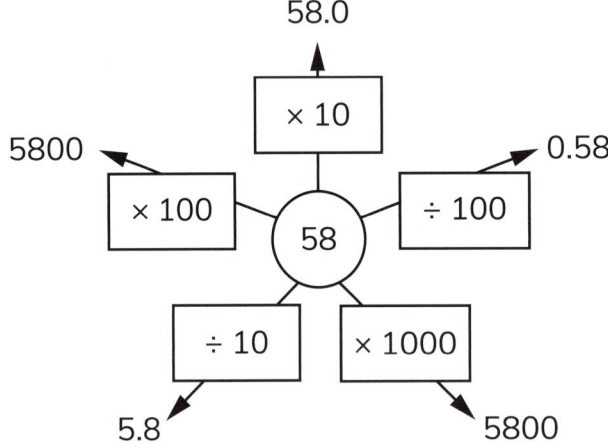

  9 Which missing number is the odd one out?

   A 33 ÷ 10 = ☐   B ☐ × 100 = 330

   C ☐ × 10 = 30.3   D 3300 ÷ 1000 = ☐

   Explain your answer.

1.2 Rounding decimal numbers

> Look back over your answers. Did you use the worked example to help you? Did you find any question particularly hard? Why?

Think like a mathematician

Zara is thinking of a decimal number less than 1.

The hundredths digit is four more than the tenths digit. The sum of the tenths digit and the hundredths digit is 10.

What number is Zara thinking of?

Make up a similar question to test your partner.

You will show you are **specialising** when you identify examples that fit the given criteria.

Look what I can do!

☐ I can explain the value of a digit in a decimal number (tenths and hundredths).

☐ I can multiply and divide whole numbers by 1000.

☐ I can multiply and divide decimals by 10 and 100.

> 1.2 Rounding decimal numbers

We are going to …

- round numbers with 1 decimal place to the nearest whole number.

Rounding makes it easier to describe and understand numbers. It is easier to understand 'an African elephant is approximately 3 metres tall' than 'the average height of an African elephant is 3.3 metres'.

nearest   round
round to the nearest …

15

1 The number system

Can you round these heights to the nearest whole number?

Height of elephant 3.3 m

Height of giraffe 5.5 m

Height of ostrich 2.7 m

How tall are you?

Worked example 2

Round these measurements to the nearest whole number.

a 3.9 m   b 4.5 m   c 0.4 m

You can use a number line to help you.

Answer:

a 4 m

b 5 m

c 0 m

If the tenths digit is 0, 1, 2, 3 or 4, round down to the nearest whole number.

If the tenths digit is 5, 6, 7, 8 or 9, round up to the nearest whole number.

1.2 Rounding decimal numbers

Exercise 1.2

1. Identify the numbers marked by arrows. Round each number to the nearest whole number.

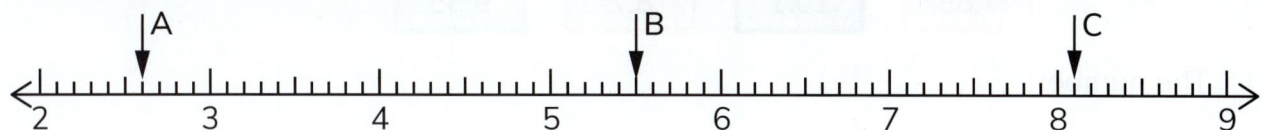

2. Round these numbers to the nearest whole number.

   a 65.8
   b 101.1
   c 44.4
   d 55.5

3. Round these measures to the nearest whole centimetre.

   a 2.8 cm
   b 8.5 cm

   Round these measures to the nearest whole metre.

   c 7.3 m
   d 0.3 m

4. A number with 1 decimal place is rounded to the nearest whole number.

   a What is the smallest number that rounds to 5?

   b What is the largest number that rounds to 5?

   Ask your partner to check your answers. Did you both choose the same numbers?

5.

   74.5 is 74 to the nearest whole number.

   Is Marcus correct?

   Explain your answer.

6. Use a calculator to help you answer this question.

   Two numbers each with 1 decimal place round to 231 to the nearest whole number.

   The sum of the two numbers is 462.

   What could the numbers be?

17

1 The number system

7 Use the clues to identify the correct number.

| 10.42 | 9.73 | 9.9 | 9.37 |
| 7.83 | 10.1 | 8.7 | 9.55 |

The number:
- has no hundredths digit
- has a tenths digit which is odd
- rounds to 10 to the nearest whole number
- is less than 10.

Swap books with your partner and check their answers.

Think about the questions you have just answered. If you were asked similar questions, what would you do differently?

Think like a mathematician

Roll a dice twice and make a number with 1 decimal place.

Find all the different numbers you can make.

Round each of your numbers to the nearest whole number.

2.5 rounds to 3
5.2 rounds to 5

Roll the dice again and make some more numbers.
What numbers with 1 decimal place are possible?
Find all the possible numbers these could round to.

Look what I can do!

☐ I can round numbers with 1 decimal place to the nearest whole number.

1.2 Rounding decimal numbers

Check your progress

1 What is the value of the digit 3 in these numbers?
   a 6703.46
   b 7021.83
   c 606 456.35

2 Write these numbers in words and digits.
   a 100 000 + 3000 + 500 + 7 + 0.9
   b 600 000 + 60 000 + 600 + 6 + 0.06

3 a What number is ten times bigger than 0.03?
   b What number is one hundred times smaller than 555?

4 Round these lengths to the nearest whole number.
   a 5.1 m
   b 16.5 cm
   c 10.4 m
   d 10.7 cm

5 Look at these number cards.

   A 450 000   B 45 000   C 4500   D 450
   E 45   F 4.5   G 0.45

   Write the letter of the card that is one hundredth of 45.

6 Write the missing numbers.
   a ☐ ÷ 1000 = 20
   b 543 × 1000 = ☐ × 10

7 What is the missing number?
   100 × 10 = 10 000 ÷ ☐

8 Sofia, Arun, Marcus and Zara each think of a number.

   Their numbers are 3.5, 0.35, 35 and 0.53.

   Use these clues to find the number each is thinking of.
   - Arun's number is ten times smaller than Marcus's number.
   - Zara's number is **not** ten times smaller than Sofia's or Arun's or Marcus's numbers.
   - Sofia's number is ten times smaller than Arun's number.

Project 1 Decimal dice

Project 1

Decimal dice

Sofia and Arun are playing a dice game. They take it in turns to roll the dice and decide which of their four boxes to put the number in. They continue until they have filled all the boxes. The aim of the game is to be the person with the number closer to 400.

At the end of the game, Sofia has the number 512.3 and Arun has 351.5.

> Who has won this game? How do you know?

Try playing this game with your partner.

> What strategies can you use to make it more likely that you will win?

Sofia and Arun are now playing a slightly different dice game. Using the same boxes, they take it in turns to roll the dice and put the number in one of their boxes until all the boxes are filled, as before. However, before they work out who the winner is, they each multiply their number by ten. The person who now has the number closer to 4000 is the winner.

Play this game a few times with your partner.

> How is it different from the first game?

Sofia and Arun want to make the game more exciting. This time, the person who rolls the dice can choose to keep the number and put it in one of their own boxes, or they can give the number to their partner and tell them which box to put it in.

Have a go at playing this new version of the game.

> Which numbers are you choosing to keep and which are you choosing to give to your partner? Why?

2 2D shape and pattern

Getting started

1. Which of these shapes are polygons?

   A B C D E

2. How many right angles does this shape have?

3. Draw a tessellating pattern using rectangles.

4. How many lines of symmetry does a square have?

2 2D shape and pattern

In this unit you will learn about triangles, tessellation, symmetry and patterns.

What triangles, tessellation, symmetry and patterns can you see in the construction of this bridge?

> 2.1 Triangles

We are going to …

- learn the names and properties of different triangles
- sketch different triangles.

Triangles are very important polygons.

They are useful when studying other shapes in mathematics because all polygons can be broken down into triangles.

Triangles are also used in architecture and building because of their strong shape.

What buildings and structures have you seen that use triangles? Describe them.

> equilateral triangle
> isosceles triangle
> scalene triangle

2 2D shape and pattern

> **Worked example 1**
>
> Is this an equilateral, isosceles or scalene triangle?

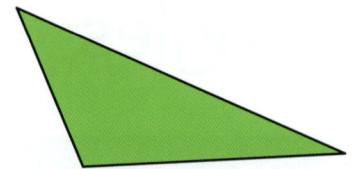

- Are all the lengths the same?

  No, the triangle is not equilateral.

- Are two of the lengths the same?

  No, the triangle is not isosceles.

- Are all the lengths different?

  Yes.

- Compare the three angles of the triangle. Are any of the angles the same size?

  No, the triangle is not equilateral or isosceles.

Measure the lengths of each side.

- All the sides of an equilateral triangle are the same length and all the angles are the same size.
- Two sides of an isosceles triangle are the same length and two of the angles are the same size.
- None of the sides of a scalene triangle are the same length and none of the angles are the same size.

Answer: The triangle is scalene.

Exercise 2.1

 1 Which of these triangles are scalene?

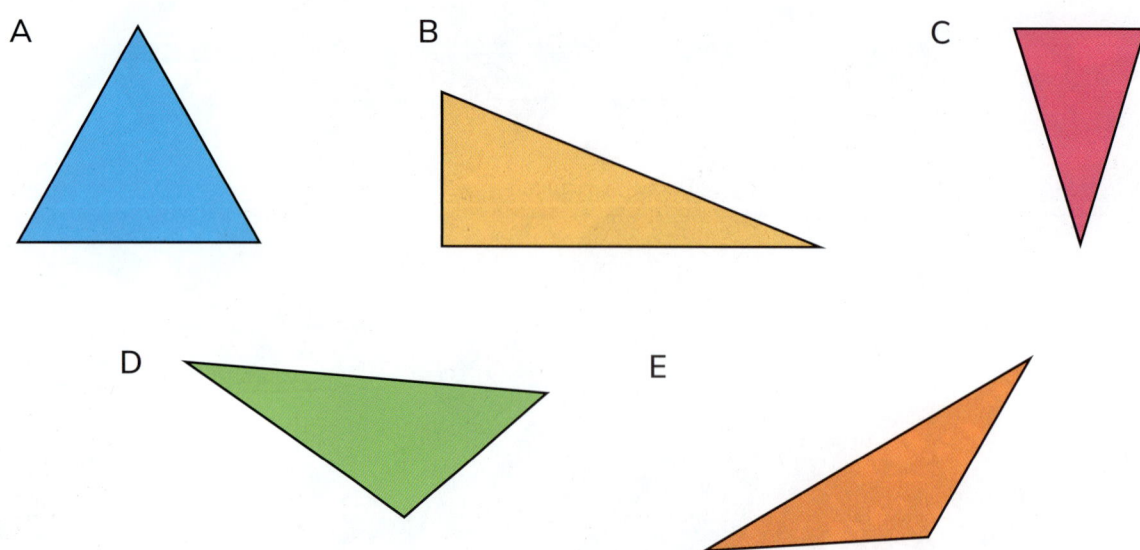

2.1 Triangles

 2 Name each type of triangle.

a 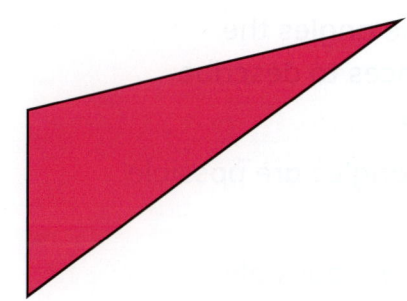 b  c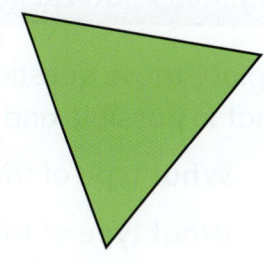

d 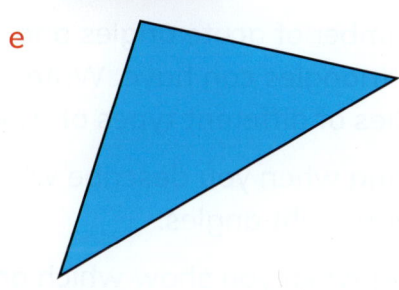 e

3 a Use a pencil and ruler to sketch an isosceles triangle.

b Use a pencil and ruler to sketch a scalene triangle.

c Ask your partner to check the triangles you have drawn in parts **a** and **b**. Check your partner's triangles by tracing and comparing the sizes of the angles. Tell your partner how you know if their triangles are isosceles and scalene.

Look at the triangles you have drawn. Think about how you drew each triangle. Most people find that an equilateral triangle is more difficult to draw. Try to draw an equilateral triangle. Think about why it might be more difficult to draw.

 4 Which of these triangles has an obtuse angle?

A 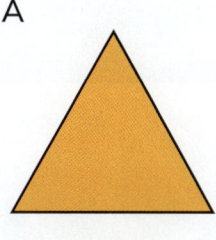 B

C 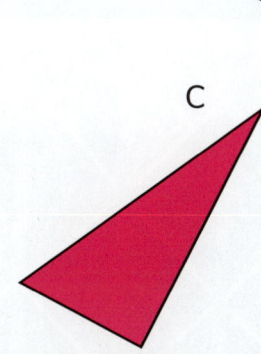 D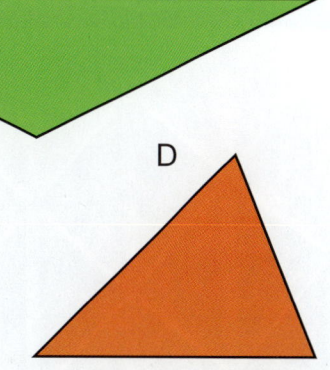

25

2　2D shape and pattern

> **Think like a mathematician**
>
> Explore these questions by drawing triangles and diagrams to show what is possible and what is impossible.
>
> a What type of triangle can have a right angle?
>
> b What type of triangle can have two right angles?
>
> c What type of triangle can have three right angles?
>
> d Investigate the number of acute angles and obtuse angles the different types of triangles can have. Write sentences to describe the angle properties of different types of triangles.
>
> - You are **generalising** when you describe which triangles are possible with each number of right angles.
>
> - You are **convincing** when you show which angles are possible and which are impossible in different triangles.

5   Name the smallest triangle that has been tessellated in each pattern.

a 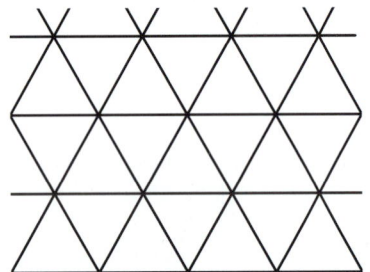   b 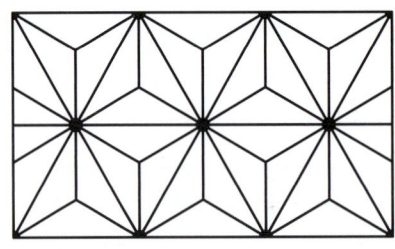   c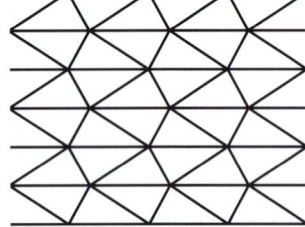

6   Is it possible to draw a triangle that cannot be tessellated?

> **Look what I can do!**
>
> ☐ I can say the names and properties of different triangles.
>
> ☐ I can sketch different triangles.

> 2.2 Symmetry

> **We are going to ...**
> - explore the symmetry in triangles
> - explore the symmetry in patterns
> - create patterns with lines of symmetry.

Symmetry is all around you in nature and in art and design. In this section you will learn how to create symmetrical patterns. Learning about symmetry helps you to notice similarity, difference and balance, which is important to all parts of mathematics.

> **line of symmetry**
> **symmetrical**

2 2D shape and pattern

Worked example 2

How many lines of symmetry does this pattern have?

Is there a vertical line of symmetry?

No, the colours are different.

Place a small mirror exactly through the middle of the pattern vertically.

Does the pattern have one side that exactly mirrors the other?

Is there a horizontal line of symmetry?

No, the colours are different.

Place a small mirror exactly through the middle of the pattern horizontally.

Does the pattern have one side that exactly mirrors the other?

2.2 Symmetry

> **Continued**
>
> Is there a diagonal line of symmetry?
>
>
>
> Place a small mirror exactly through the middle of the pattern along different diagonals.
>
> Does the pattern have one side that exactly mirrors the other?
>
> No, the colours are different.
>
> **Answer:** The pattern has 0 lines of symmetry.

Exercise 2.2

1 How many lines of symmetry does each triangle have?

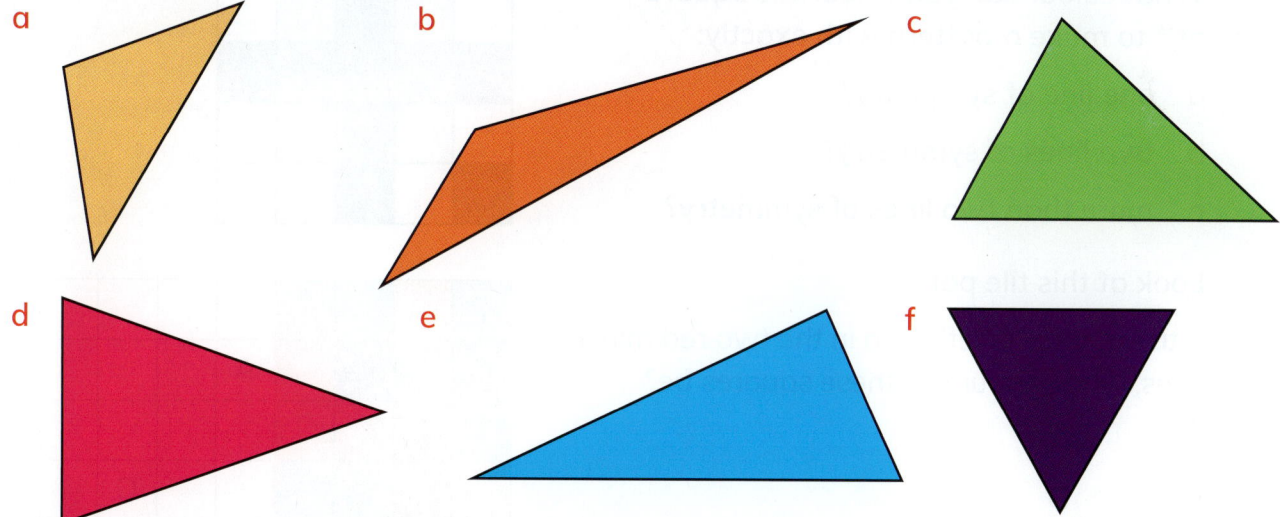

Check with your partner. Do you get the same answers?

Use a mirror to check for lines of symmetry and to find any that you missed.

Write a sentence to say how good you are at finding lines of symmetry in triangles and how you can improve.

2 2D shape and pattern

2 These tiles have reflective symmetry in their shape and in their patterns. How many lines of symmetry does each pattern have?

a

b

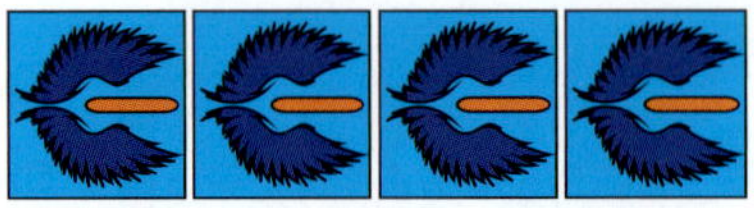

c

d

e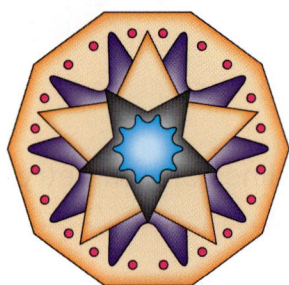

3 Look at this pattern.

What colour can you colour the square at * to make a pattern with exactly:

a one line of symmetry?

b two lines of symmetry?

c more than two lines of symmetry?

4 Look at this tile pattern.

If the pattern is reflected in the two red mirror lines, what colour will these squares be?

A   B
C   D
E   F
G

Copy the pattern onto squared paper and colour the rest of the pattern as it will look when it is reflected in the two mirror lines.

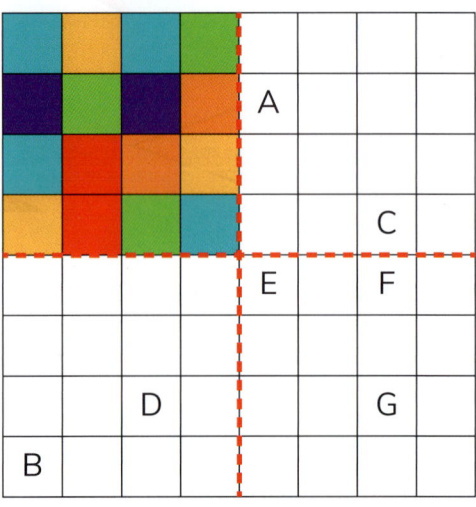

2.2 Symmetry

5 Copy and complete this pattern by reflecting the shapes over both mirror lines until there are three shapes in each quadrant.

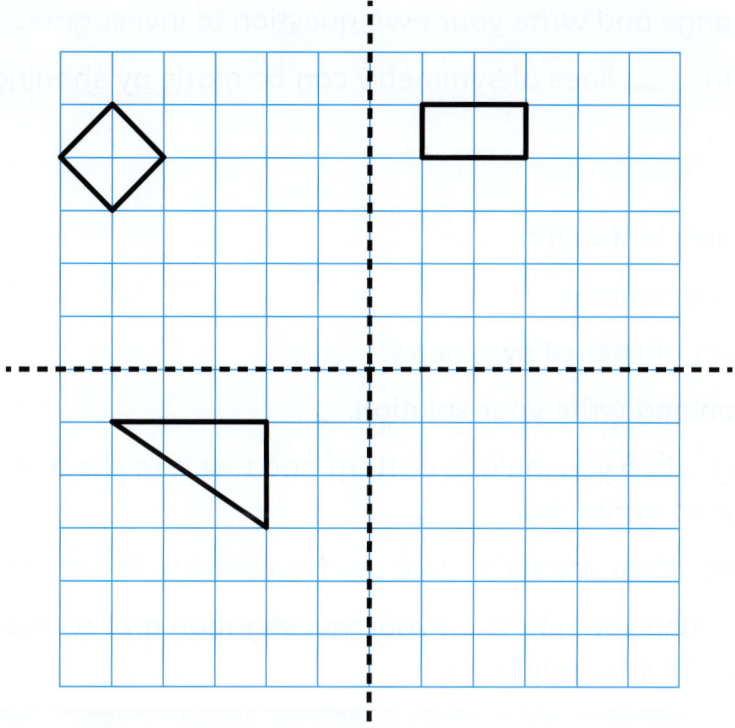

Think like a mathematician

This is a square grid of 9 squares.

Use one colour pen or pencil and squared paper.

How many patterns with at least 1 line of symmetry can you make by shading 4 squares?

Try not to make patterns that look the same from different directions.

For example, these two patterns are the same.

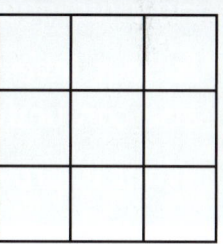

 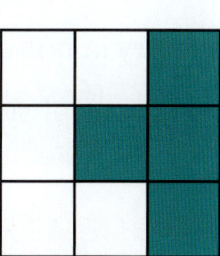

2 2D shape and pattern

> **Continued**
>
> Choose **one** thing to change and write your own question to investigate.
>
> How many patterns with _____ lines of symmetry can be made by shading _____ squares?
>
> You could change:
> - the number of squares in the grid
> - the number of shaded squares
> - the minimum number of lines of symmetry.
>
> Investigate your question and write your solution.
>
> - You are **specialising** when you make a pattern and test it to check if it has at least one line of symmetry.
> - You are **conjecturing** when you write your own question to investigate.
> - You are **improving** when you reflect on your investigation and consider how you could improve your approach.

Look at your investigation.
- How did you make sure that you did not repeat patterns?
- Is your investigation clear and organised so that someone else can understand what you did and what you found out?
- What improvements could you make?

Look what I can do!

☐ I can describe the symmetry in triangles.

☐ I can describe the symmetry in patterns.

☐ I can create patterns with lines of symmetry.

Check your progress

1. Draw an isosceles triangle with one side that is longer than the other two sides.
2. Which of these triangles are equilateral?

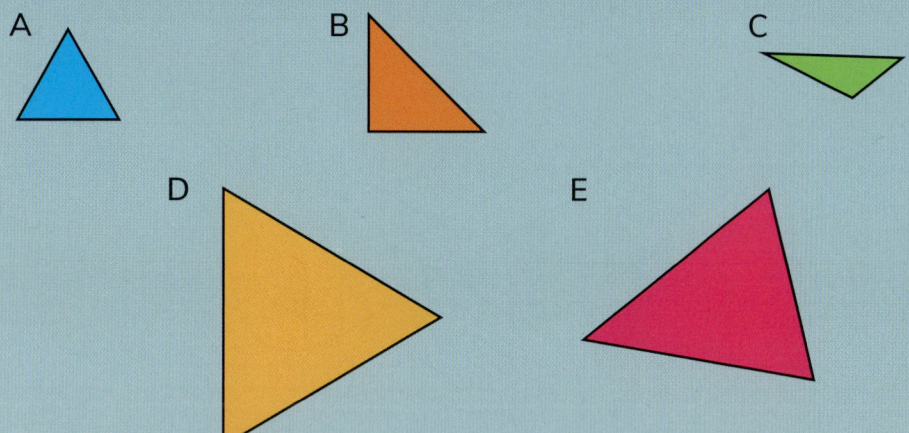

3. Which types of triangle can be used to make a tessellating pattern?
4. How many lines of symmetry does an equilateral triangle have?
5. Here are two rangoli patterns.
   How many lines of symmetry does each pattern have?

   a

2 2D shape and pattern

Continued

b

6   Copy this grid onto squared paper for each part of this question.

a   Colour the grid so that there are no lines of symmetry.

b   Colour the grid so that there is exactly 1 line of symmetry.

c   Colour the grid so that there are exactly 2 lines of symmetry.

d   Colour the grid so that there are exactly 4 lines of symmetry.

3 Numbers and sequences

Getting started

1. A sequence starts at 16.

   3 is subtracted each time.

   What is the first number in the sequence that is less than zero?

2. Here is a number sequence. It continues in the same way.

   516, 616, 716, 816, ...

   a What is the term-to-term rule for continuing the sequence?

   b What are the next two terms in the sequence?

3. a Draw the next term in this sequence.

   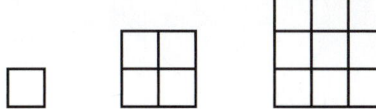

   b What is the mathematical name for these numbers?

4. Find a 2-digit number that satisfies all these rules:
   - It is a multiple of 3.
   - It is a multiple of 4.
   - It ends in 6.

3 Numbers and sequences

This unit is all about patterns and sequences. You will look at linear sequences and non-linear sequences, square numbers, triangular numbers, prime numbers and composite numbers.

Imagine you are making pancakes using a pancake mix.

The number of pancakes in the second column of the table is a linear sequence.

Cups of pancake mix	Number of pancakes
1	8
2	16
3	24

The term-to-term rule is 'add 8'.

How many cups of pancake mix do you need to make 40 pancakes?

Can you think of some patterns and sequences in the environment or your everyday life?

Here are two to get you thinking.

> 3.1 Counting and sequences

> **We are going to …**
> - count on and count back in steps of constant size including counting back through zero to include using negative numbers
> - find the jump size for a linear sequence and relate this to multiplication.

A lighthouse displays a single flash repeated at regular times.

It can also display groups of two, three or four flashes with spaces between the groups.

The whole pattern is repeated at regular intervals.

In this section you will learn about sequences that follow particular rules.

> linear sequence
> sequence
> term
> term-to-term rule

Worked example 1

a Write the first four terms of a sequence with first term 1 and term-to-term rule 'add 4'.

b Find the 10th term.

Answer:

a 1, 5, 9, 13

Position number	Term
1	1
2	5
3	9
4	13

+4
+4
+4

b The 10th term is: To find the 10th term start at 1 and then add 9 jumps of 4.

$1 + 9 \times 4 = 37$

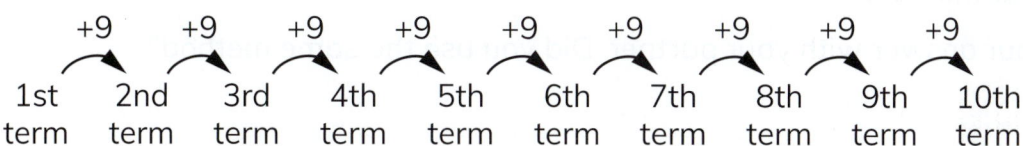

+9 +9 +9 +9 +9 +9 +9 +9 +9

1st 2nd 3rd 4th 5th 6th 7th 8th 9th 10th
term term term term term term term term term term

37

3 Numbers and sequences

Exercise 3.1

1   a   Here is a sequence made of sticks.
        Draw the next pattern in the sequence.

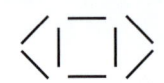

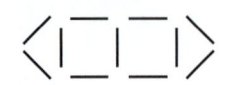

    b   Copy and complete the table.

    c   Find the term-to-term rule.

    d   How many sticks are in the 10th pattern?

Pattern number	Number of sticks
1	
2	
3	
4	

    Discuss your answers with your partner.

2   a   Write the first four terms of a sequence with first term 1 and term-to-term rule 'add 11'.

    b   Find the 15th term.

3   A sequence starts at 40 and 9 is subtracted each time.

    40, 31, 22, ...

    What are the first two numbers in the sequence that are less than zero?

4   Pierre starts counting at 88 and counts back in steps of 8.

    88, 80, 72, 64, ...

    Will the number 1 be in the sequence?

    How can you tell without counting back?

5   Sofia makes a number sequence.

    The first term is 155 and the term-to-term rule is 'subtract 7'.

    Sofia says, 'If I keep subtracting 7 from 155, I will eventually reach 0.'

    Is she correct? Explain your answer.

6   The numbers in this sequence increase by equal amounts each time.

    Copy the sequence and write in the missing numbers.

    1, ▢, ▢, 7

    Explain your method.

    Discuss your answer with your partner. Did you use the same method?

3.1 Counting and sequences

7 Marcus writes a sequence of numbers.
   His rule is to add the same amount each time.
   Copy the sequence and write in the missing numbers.

   1, ☐, ☐, ☐, 21

> Think back over the work you have done on sequences.
> What have you learned? Is there anything you need to get better at?

Think like a mathematician

You can write a sequence with a constant jump size if you know three pieces of information:

- the first term
- the jump size
- the number of terms in the sequence.

This information is given in the table for five sequences.

Write each of the sequences A to E.

	First term (number)	Jump size	Number of terms in the sequence
A	1	+4	5
B	20	−3	5
C	−15	+11	5
D	100	−26	5
E	−40	+15	5

Make up some linear sequences of your own and write down the three pieces of information that define your sequences.

You will show you are **specialising** when you find sequences that satisfy the given criteria.

Look what I can do!

☐ I can count on and count back in steps of constant size including counting back through zero to include using negative numbers.

☐ I can find the jump size for a linear sequence and relate this to multiplication.

3 Numbers and sequences

> 3.2 Square and triangular numbers

> **We are going to …**
>
> - learn to recognise and extend spatial patterns that represent square numbers and triangular numbers
> - learn to recognise square numbers from 1 to 100.

Look at these examples of patterns of squares.

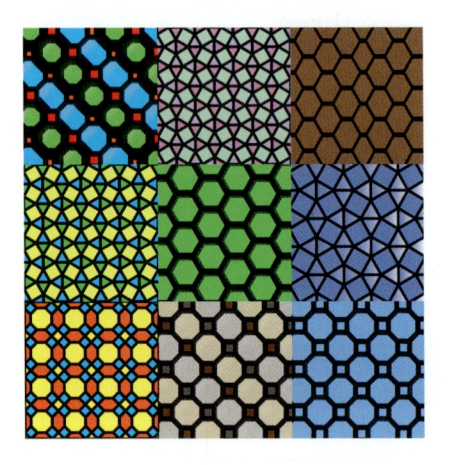

Look along the diagonal of this table square.

What do you notice?

×	1	2	3	4	5	6
1	1	2	3	4	5	6
2	2	4	6	8	10	12
3	3	6	9	12	15	18
4	4	8	12	16	20	24
5	5	10	15	20	25	30
6	6	12	18	24	30	36

> spatial pattern
> square number
> triangular number

In this section, you will learn about two number sequences: square numbers and triangular numbers.

40

3.2 Square and triangular numbers

Worked example 2

Look at these patterns made from squares.

The sequence starts 1, 4, 9, ...

a Draw the next term in the sequence.

b Write the next three numbers in the sequence.

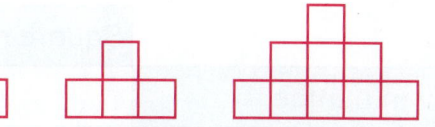

Answer:

a

Look carefully at the pattern to see how it is made. In this case, in each term, there is an extra row which has two more squares than the row before.

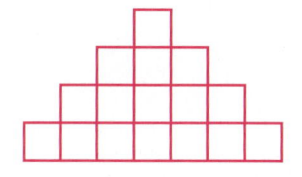

b 16, 25, 36

Look at the numbers you have for the first four terms in the sequence. Can you see a pattern?

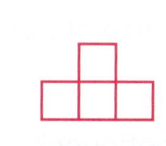

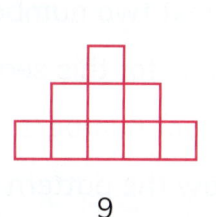

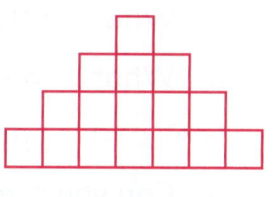

1	4	9	16
1	1 + 3 = 4	1 + 3 + 5 = 9	1 + 3 + 5 + 7 = 16
1	1 + 3	4 + 5 = 9	9 + 7 = 16
$1 \times 1 = 1$	$2 \times 2 = 4$	$3 \times 3 = 9$	$4 \times 4 = 16$
$1^2 = 1$	$2^2 = 4$	$3^2 = 9$	$4^2 = 16$

Exercise 3.2

1 These patterns of dots show the first four square numbers.

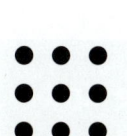

   a Draw a dot pattern for the 5th square number.

   b What is the 10th square number?

3 Numbers and sequences

2 Copy and complete the Carroll diagram by writing a number greater than 50 but less than 100 in each space.

	Square number	Not a square number
Even number		
Not an even number		

Discuss your answer with your partner.
There are lots of possible answers.

3 Look at this number pattern made using counters.

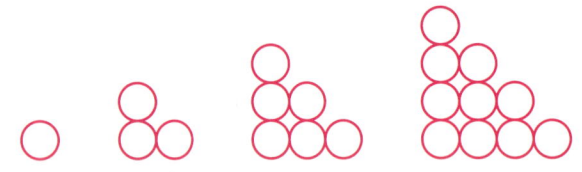

The pattern starts 1, 3, 6, 10.

a What are the next two numbers in the sequence?

b What is the name for this sequence of numbers?

4 Look at this pattern of numbers.

a Can you see how the pattern continues?

Discuss your ideas with a partner and then draw the next two rows of the triangle.

b Find the sum of the numbers in each row, then write down the first eight numbers in the sequence.

1, 2, 4, ☐, ☐, ☐, ☐, ☐

c Describe the sequence.

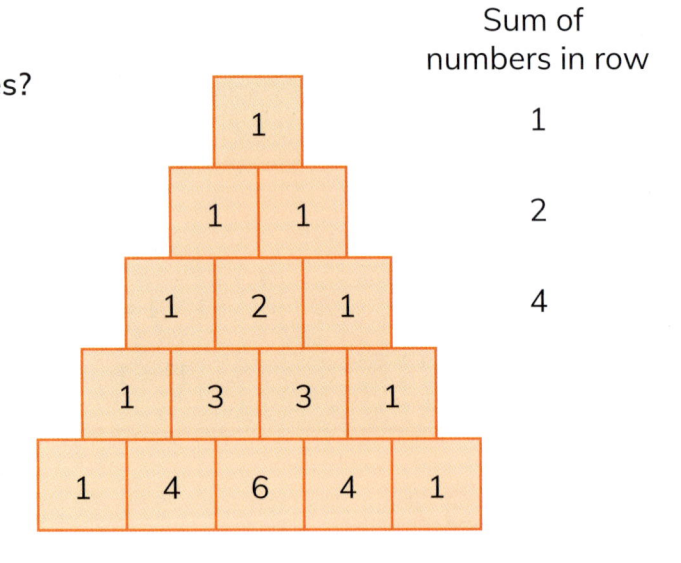

Sum of numbers in row

1 — 1
1 1 — 2
1 2 1 — 4
1 3 3 1
1 4 6 4 1

5 Calculate these square numbers.

a 6^2 b 8^2 c 9^2

Have you ever thought that some numbers are both square and triangular? The number 1 is both.

If you continue the sequence you found in question 3 to the 8th term you will find another number that is both square and triangular.

42

3.3 Prime and composite numbers

> **Think like a mathematician**
>
> You can multiply 15 by itself to give a 3-digit number.
>
> | 1 | 5 | × | 1 | 5 | = | 2 | 2 | 5 |
>
> What is the **smallest** 2-digit number that you can multiply by itself to give a 3-digit number?
>
> Use a calculator to investigate the **largest** 2-digit number that you can multiply by itself to give a 3-digit number?
>
> ☐☐ × ☐☐ = ☐☐☐
>
> - You will show you are **specialising** when you find numbers that satisfy the given criteria.
> - If you explain your results, you will show you are **convincing**.

Look what I can do!

☐ I can recognise and extend spatial patterns that represent square and triangular numbers.

☐ I can recognise square numbers from 1 to 100.

> 3.3 Prime and composite numbers

We are going to ...

- find prime numbers up to 100
- understand the difference between prime and composite numbers.

You already know how to find factors of numbers.

Some special numbers have exactly two factors. For example:

- 3 has factors 1 and 3
- 7 has factors 1 and 7.

> composite number
> factor
> multiple
> prime number

43

3 Numbers and sequences

These special numbers are called prime numbers. Can you think of any other prime numbers?

Prime numbers are very important! Adults often buy goods online using a credit card. Every time they send a credit card number over the internet, it is converted into a code which is based on prime numbers!

Worked example 3

Write a different prime number in each box to make this calculation correct.

☐ + ☐ + ☐ = 10

The prime numbers are:	Start by writing a list of prime numbers.
2, 3, 5, 7, …	Test different numbers to work out which ones make the calculation correct.
2 + 3 + 5 = 10	When you test numbers like this you are **specialising**.

Exercise 3.3

1. Which of these numbers are prime numbers?

    11   21   31   41   51   61

    How do you know they are prime numbers?

2. Which number could be the odd one out?

    19   39   49

    Give two different answers and explain your reason.

3. Copy and complete this sentence.

    A number with more than two factors is called a ____ number.

3.3 Prime and composite numbers

4   Copy this Venn diagram and write each number in the correct place.

15   16   17   18   19

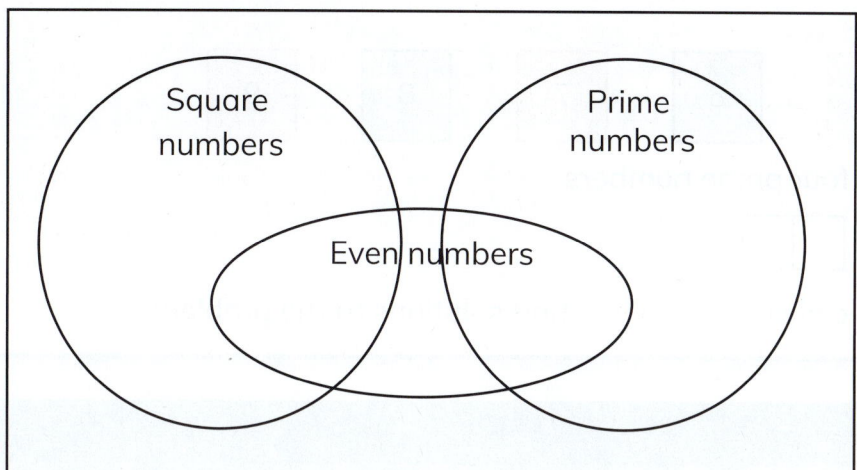

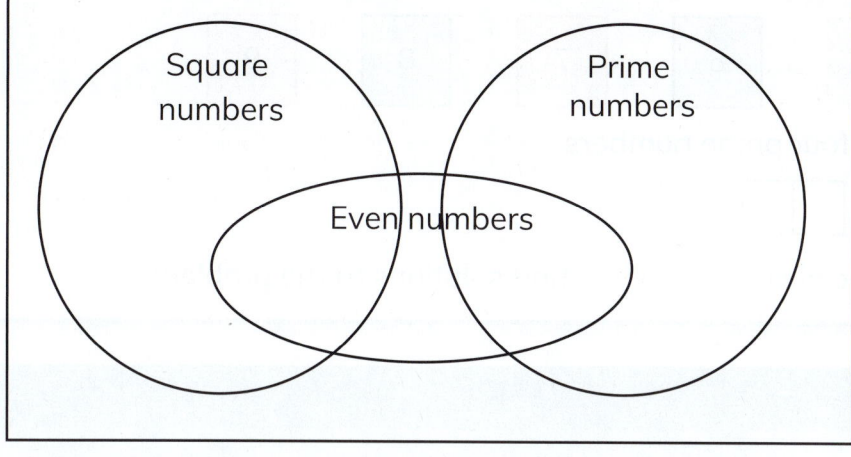

(Venn diagram with three overlapping sets: Square numbers, Prime numbers, and Even numbers)

5   Arun and Zara play a game of 'What's my number?'

Arun says:	Zara replies:
Is the number less than 20?	No
Is the number less than 25?	Yes
Is the number even?	No
Is the number prime?	Yes

What is the number?

6   Here are four digit cards.

1   2   5   9

Choose two cards each time to make the following 2-digit numbers.

a   A prime number

b   A multiple of 3

c   A square number

d   A factor of 36

Discuss your answers with your partner.

Think about the different types of numbers you have learned about in this unit. Are you confident that you can give a definition and find examples of a square, triangular and prime number?

In Stage 6, you will learn about cube numbers. What do you think a cube number is?

3 Numbers and sequences

Think like a mathematician

Here are some digit cards.

| 2 | 3 | 5 | 6 | 7 | 8 | 9 |

Use all the cards to make four prime numbers.

☐ ☐☐ ☐☐ ☐☐

You will show you are **specialising** when you find solutions to the problem.

Look what I can do!

☐ I can find prime numbers up to 100.

☐ I understand the difference between prime and composite numbers.

Check your progress

1. Sofia wrote a list of three square numbers.
   Which of these is Sofia's list?

   A 9, 10, 11   B 9, 19, 29   C 9, 16, 25   D 9, 99, 999

2. Given the first term and the term-to-term rule, write down the first six terms of each sequence.

   a First term is 7, term-to-term rule is 'add 6'.
   b First term is 2, term-to-term rule is 'add 7'.

3. The numbers in this sequence increase by equal amounts each time.
   What are the three missing numbers?

   1, ☐, ☐, ☐, 13

4. Zara counts in sevens starting at 1.

   1, 8, 15, 22, 29, …

   Zara continues counting in this way.
   Will she say the number 77? Explain how you know.

5. Marcus is thinking of a prime number between 1 and 20.
   He says, 'If I add 1 to my number it is a multiple of 9.'
   What number is Marcus thinking of?

Project 2: Pattern prediction

> Project 2

Pattern prediction

Marcus and Zara were asked to draw this matchstick pattern:

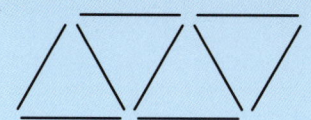

Marcus drew this first:

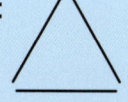

Then he added more to make this:

Then this:

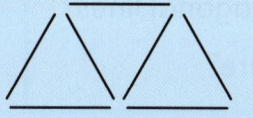

Then finally:

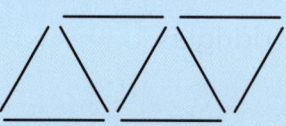

> Can you describe how Marcus drew the pattern?
>
> How many triangles did he draw?
>
> How many matchsticks did he use in the finished picture?

Now picture what Marcus would draw if there were 10 triangles.

How many matchsticks would this use?

What about if there were 101 triangles?

47 >

Project 2 Pattern prediction

Continued

Zara also drew the pattern. First she drew this:

Then this:

Then finally:

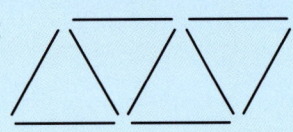

> Can you describe how Zara drew the pattern?
>
> How many horizontal lines did she draw? How many diagonal lines?
>
> How many matchsticks did she use in the finished picture?

Now picture what Zara would draw if there were 10 triangles.

How many horizontal lines would she draw?

How many diagonal lines?

How many matchsticks would this use altogether?

What about if there were 101 triangles?

Now look at this pattern of three 'houses'.

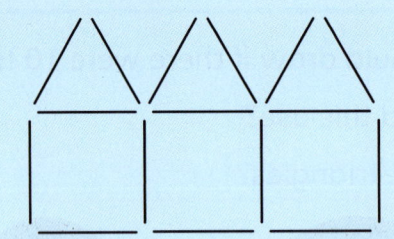

Try to picture how to make the next, and the next, and the next …

Use this to help you find the total number of matchsticks used for the pattern with 10 houses.

What about the pattern with 101 houses?

Can you explain your reasoning?

4 Averages

Getting started

1. Which pencil is in the middle?

2. Write these sets of numbers in order from smallest to greatest.

   a 3, 7, 9, 4, 1, 5, 8

   b 14, 401, 114, 414, 41, 144, 104

3. Imagine you take a piece from this bag without looking.

   Which shape are you most likely to take? Why?

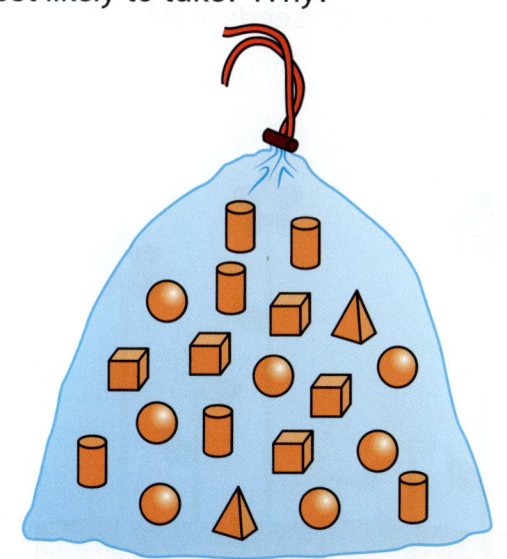

4 Averages

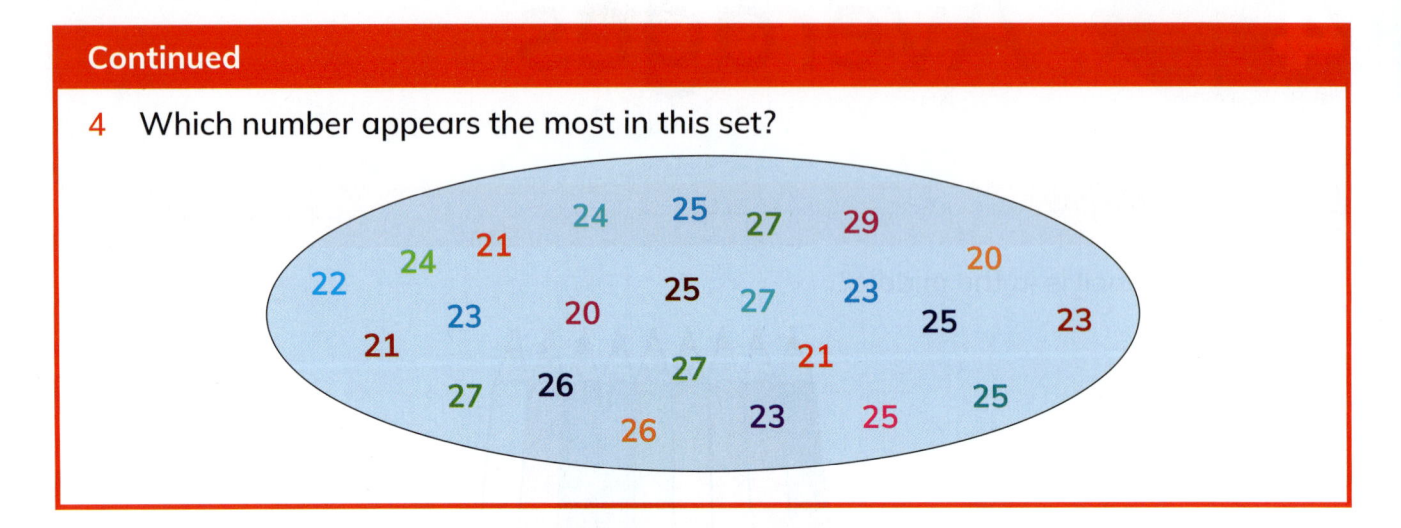

> **Continued**
>
> 4 Which number appears the most in this set?
>
> 22 24 21 24 25 27 29 20
> 21 23 20 25 27 23 25 23
>   27 26 27 21 25
>   26 23 25

You can use averages to help you understand data in real life. Averages can tell you things like the most common score or height. Averages can tell you about the most popular flavour. They can also help you work out what thing is most likely to happen.

In this unit you will learn about two types of average called the mode and the median.

These seed packets tell you the average height of the dark blue and light yellow flowers.

Which packet do you think had which seeds in it?

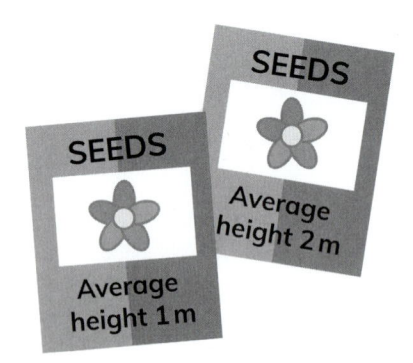

SEEDS — Average height 1 m

SEEDS — Average height 2 m

50

> 4.1 Mode and median

> **We are going to …**
>
> - learn about the mode of a set of data
> - learn about the median of a set of data
> - compare the mode and the median to find an average that describes a set of data in context.

Averages can help you solve problems and make decisions. When people give a film a score out of 10, all their scores can be put together to find an average score.

Look at this film score:

Film Review

The Fun Film   Average score 6 out of 10.

> average
> median
> mode

Not everybody gave the film 6 out of 10.

Some people might have given a score or 1 out of 10, or 10 out of 10!

The average represents what many people think about the film when their reviews are all put together. You can use the average score to help you decide if you want to see the film.

Would you watch the film? Why?

In this section you will learn two ways to work out the average of a set of data.

4 Averages

Exercise 4.1

1 What is the mode of these sets of numbers?

   a 1, 1, 1, 2, 3

   b 30, 29, 31, 29, 32

   c 8, 9, 9, 8, 9, 8, 9

   d $1\frac{1}{2}, 1\frac{1}{4}, 1\frac{1}{2}, 1\frac{3}{4}, 1\frac{3}{4}, 1\frac{3}{4}$

2 These are the number of bananas in each bunch in a shop.

   6   4   5   6   7   4   4   5   6   5   7   5

   What is the mode of the number of bananas in a bunch?

> **Tip**
>
> The value which occurs the most often is the mode. For example, here is a set of animals: cat, cat, mouse, rabbit. 'Cat' occurs the most so 'cat' is the mode.

Worked example 1

What is the median of these heights?

133 cm, 137 cm, 134 cm, 131 cm, 132 cm

131 cm, 132 cm, 133 cm, 134 cm, 137 cm	Write the heights in order from smallest to greatest.
~~131 cm~~, 132 cm, 133 cm, 134 cm, ~~137 cm~~	Cross through the first and last heights.
~~131 cm~~, ~~132 cm~~, (133 cm,) ~~134 cm~~, ~~137 cm~~	Keep crossing through the heights from the two ends of the list until you reach the middle.
Answer: The median is 133 cm.	The height in the middle is the median of the set of heights.

52

4.1 Mode and median

3   These sets of numbers are written in order.
    Find the median of each set.

    a   1, 2, 3, 4, 5

    b   5, 5, 6, 7, 7, 8, 9, 9, 9, 10, 10

    c   253, 257, 270, 299, 308, 310, 324, 740, 751

> **Tip**
>
> The median is the middle value in a sorted list of numbers.

4   These sets of numbers are not written in order. Find the median of each set.

    a   3, 7, 1, 5, 9

    b   13, 13, 11, 12, 14, 12, 14, 14, 11

    c   535, 422, 278, 567, 453, 772, 329

5   What is the median mass of these bags?

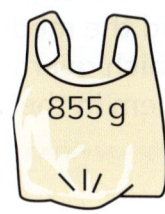

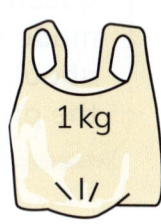

    670 g   855 g   1 kg   722 g   595 g   998 g   789 g

6   Find the mode and the median of each set of numbers.

    Copy and complete this sentence for each set:

    'The mode is ____ and the median is ____ .'

    a   5, 6, 1, 2, 6   b   11, 12, 9, 11, 11, 12, 13

    c   3, 5, 6, 2, 9, 3, 4, 3, 5   d   5, 2, 5, 6, 7, 2, 3, 2, 1

Think like a mathematician

What set of five numbers has a mode of 3 **and** a median of 3?

[?] [?] [?] [?] [?]

Write two more sets of numbers that have a mode of 3 **and** a median of 3.

Swap answers with your partner.

Check that your partner's sets have a mode of 3 and a median of 3.

You will show you are **specialising** when you find sets of numbers that satisfy the given criteria.

4 Averages

Copy and complete these sentences to explain how you check that the mode and median is 3.
- I check that the mode is 3 by ...
- I check that the median is 3 by ...

7 A shop sells gloves in sizes 1, 2, 3 and 4.

In one day the shop sells these glove sizes:

1, 2, 3, 4, 1, 4, 4, 2, 4

a What is the mode of the glove sizes sold?

b What is the median of the glove sizes sold?

c The shopkeeper wants to buy more gloves to put in the shop, but the shopkeeper can only buy one size of gloves. Should the shopkeeper use the mode or the median to decide what size gloves to buy? Why?

Tip

Sometimes one type of average is more useful than another to solve a problem. Read the question carefully. Work out the mode and the median. Think about which average best solves the problem in the question.

8 This table shows the rainfall for the first 11 months of the year.
Use the table to work out the average amount of rain in a month.

Month	Jan	Feb	Mar	Apr	May	June	July	Aug	Sept	Oct	Nov
Rainfall (mm)	7	6	14	13	5	0	4	4	0	0	3

a What is the mode amount of rain?

b What is the median amount of rain?

c Do you think that the mode or the median best describes the average monthly rainfall? Why?

Look what I can do!

☐ I can find the mode of a set of data.

☐ I can find the median of a set of data.

☐ I can compare the mode and median to find an average that describes a set of data in context.

4.1 Mode and median

Check your progress

1   What is the mode of these shoe prices?

   $30 $19.99 $18.50 $18.50 $25.45

2   What is the median length of these ribbons?

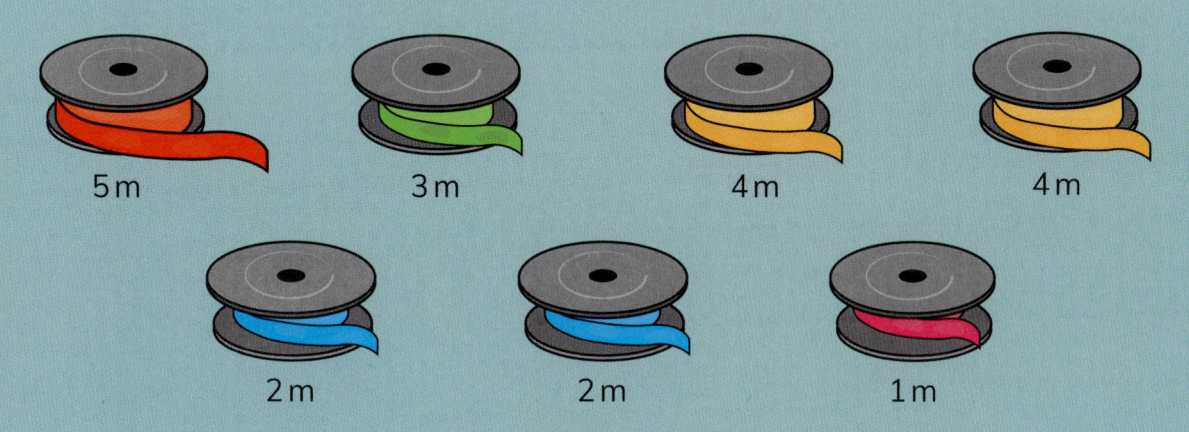

   5 m, 3 m, 4 m, 4 m, 2 m, 2 m, 1 m

3   What is the mode and the median of these sets of numbers?
   a   101, 102, 103, 103, 104, 105, 106, 106, 106
   b   3, 7, 4, 9, 6, 7, 5, 1, 2
   c   26, 26, 27, 28, 30, 31, 32, 32, 32, 31, 29
   d   2, 1, 2, 4, 3, 2, 1, 2, 3, 2, 4

4 Averages

Continued

4   Lucas has been asked to report the average amount of money raised at an event. These are the amounts of money:

$9 $7 $6 $5 $9

   a   What is the mode of the amounts?

   b   What is the median amount?

   c   Is it better to use the mode or the median to describe the average amount of money raised? Why?

5   Maryam wants to use an average to work out what size tables are most useful in her restaurant. She collects data about the size of groups of people that eat in the restaurant. These are the sizes of the groups:

3   2   4   4   1   5   4   2   2   4   1

   a   Find the mode of the data.

   b   Find the median of the data.

   c   Is it better to use the mode or the median to decide what size tables will be most useful? Why?

5 Addition and subtraction

Getting started

1. Find the missing numbers.

   a 100 − ☐ = 37

   b 131 + ☐ = 190

2. Zara describes a number.

   She says, 'My number has 6 thousands and 708 ones.'

   a Write Zara's numbers in digits and in words.

   b Regroup her number in a different way.

3. Look at these calculations.

   Explain any errors and write the correct answer.

	5	9	7
+		1	7
	6	0	4

	3	9	2
−	1	6	8
	2	3	6

4. If −6 < ☐ < −3 what whole number could ☐ represent?

5 Addition and subtraction

You are surrounded by numbers in your everyday life. They may be whole numbers, fractions, decimals, percentages or negative numbers.

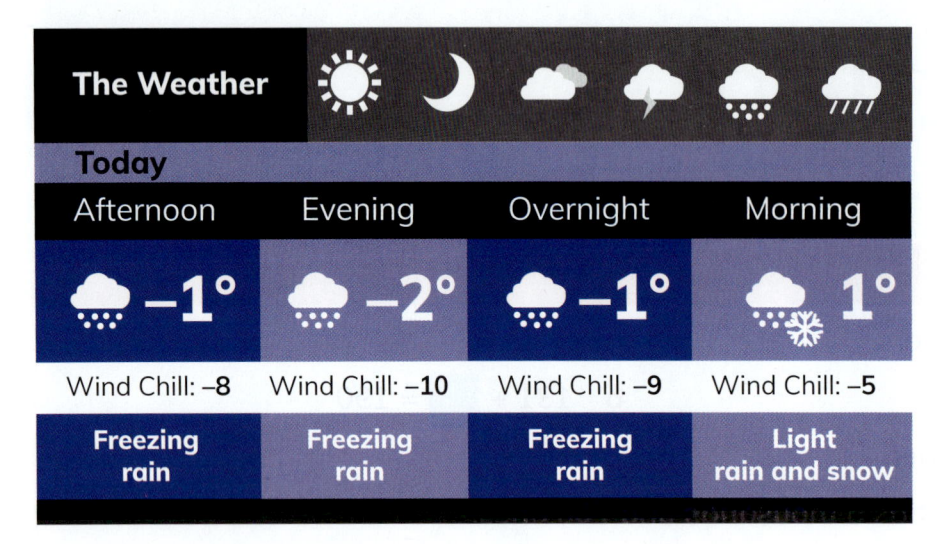

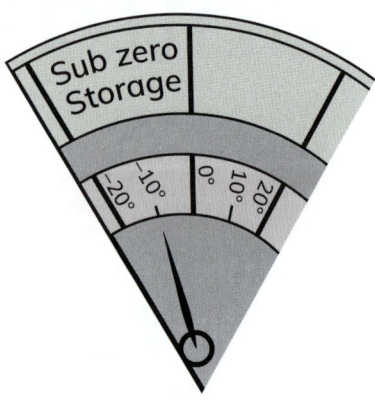

Negative numbers are used in different situations.

- In weather reports, a temperature of −5 °C means the temperature is 5 degrees below zero.

- On food packaging there might be instructions for storing food, for example, 'Store below −10 °C'.

- If you or your parents have a bank account and you spend some money, the amount you spend may show as a negative number.

This extract from a bank statement uses decimal numbers. For example, $4.50 represents $4 and 50 cents.

Date:
From: 17 Sept
To: 26 Sept

Description	Amount ($)	Balance ($)
Take out cash	−20.00	240.00
Electricity bill	−150.00	90.00
Pay in cash	4.50	94.50

> 5.1 Addition and subtraction including decimal numbers

> **We are going to ...**
> - compose, decompose and regroup numbers to help with calculation
> - estimate, add and subtract decimal numbers
> - use shapes and symbols to represent two unknown numbers in addition and subtraction calculations.

In a gymnastics competition, judges give a score for how difficult a routine is and a score for how well it is performed.

The two scores are added together to give the final total.

All the scores are decimal numbers.

> carry, carrying
> symbol

	Gymnast 1	Gymnast 2	Gymnast 3
Score 1	7.72	6.81	8.26
Score 2	9.05	8.15	9.53
Total	16.77	14.96	17.79

In this unit, you will add and subtract decimal numbers.

59

5 Addition and subtraction

> **Worked example 1**
>
> Calculate 9.75 + 13.42.
>
> Estimate: 10 + 13 = 23   Always start by estimating.
>
> **Method 1**
>
> $\quad\quad\quad 9 + 0.7 + 0.05$
> $+\ 10 + 3 + 0.4 + 0.02$
> $\overline{\quad 10 + 12 + 1.1 + 0.07}$
>
> Decompose each number into tens, ones, tenths and hundredths. Then add each column.
>
> $10 + 12 + 1.1 + 0.07 = 23.17$ Regroup to give the final answer.
>
> **Method 2**
>
> | | | 9 | . | 7 | 5 |
> |---|---|---|---|---|---|
> | + | 1 | 3 | . | 4 | 2 |
> | | 2 | 3 | . | 1 | 7 |
> | | 1 | 1 | | | |
>
> Write the calculation in columns.
>
> Use an efficient, column method with carrying.
>
> **Answer:** 9.75 + 13.42 = 23.17

Exercise 5.1

1. What decimal number is represented by 70 + 8 + 0.3 + 0.01?

2. Estimate then calculate.

   a 28.2 + 13.4   b 12.46 + 1.31   c 13.41 + 4.39
   d 28.2 − 13.8   e 123.1 − 47.3   f 34.29 − 7.41

   Compare your answers with your partner. Did you use the same method?

   Check your answers with a calculator.

5.1 Addition and subtraction including decimal numbers

3   Alana hands in her homework.

    3.4 + 1.8

		3 .	4
+		1 .	8
	4	1 .	2

    6.5 − 2.7

	6 .	5
−	2 .	7
	4 .	2

    Mark the homework and correct any errors.

    What advice would you give to Alana?

4   Fatima has $7.25. She is given $15.50

    How much does she have now?

5   In a sale, a shop takes $2.25 off the price of these books.

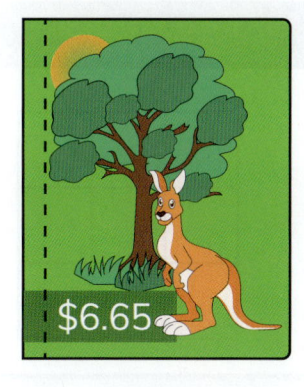

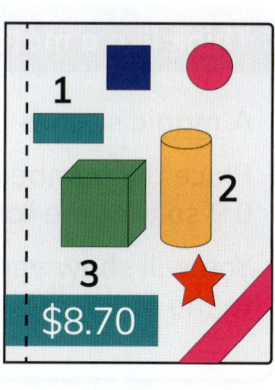

    A $6.65   B $16.35   C $15.50   D $8.70

    a   What is the cost of each book in the sale?
    b   What is the total cost of the four books in the sale?

6   a   ■ and ● each stand for a different whole number.

    ■ + ■ + ■ = 42

    ■ + ● = 23

    What is the value of each shape?

    Compare your answer with your partner.

    b   ▲ and ● each stand for a different whole number.

    ▲ + ▲ = 18

    ▲ − ● = 5

    What is the value of each shape?

5 Addition and subtraction

7 Each symbol stands for a number.
Find the value of each symbol.

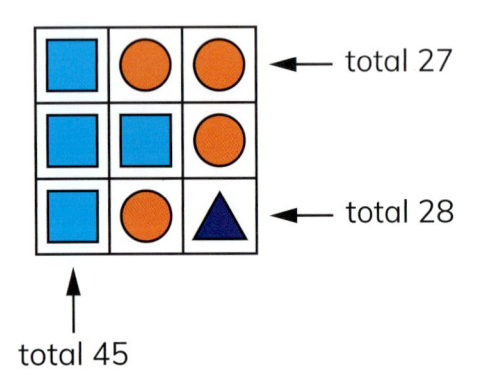

← total 27

← total 28

↑
total 45

8 What are the possible values of ■ and ▲ when

■ + ■ + ■ + ▲ = 1.3 kg?

Think like a mathematician

A magic square

Place the numbers 0.1, 0.2, 0.3, 0.4, 0.5, 0.6, 0.7, 0.8 and 0.9 so that the total of each row, column and diagonal is 1.5.

You will show you are **specialising** when you find a solution to the problem.

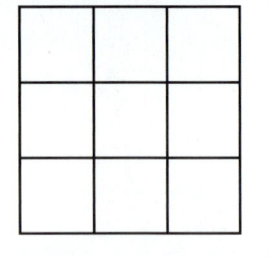

You might remember the work you did on addition and subtraction of whole numbers in previous years. How did that help you with this section?

Look what I can do!

☐ I can compose, decompose and regroup numbers to help with calculation.

☐ I can estimate, add and subtract decimal numbers.

☐ I can use shapes and symbols to represent two unknown numbers in addition and subtraction calculations.

> 5.2 Addition and subtraction of positive and negative numbers

We are going to …

- add and subtract positive and negative numbers.

If you watch the floors as you go down in an elevator, the numbers change from positive to negative.

In this building, the car park is on level −2 which is the second floor underground.

In this section you will learn to add and subtract positive and negative numbers.

integer
negative number
positive number

63

5 Addition and subtraction

> **Worked example 2**
>
> What is 6 less than 1? 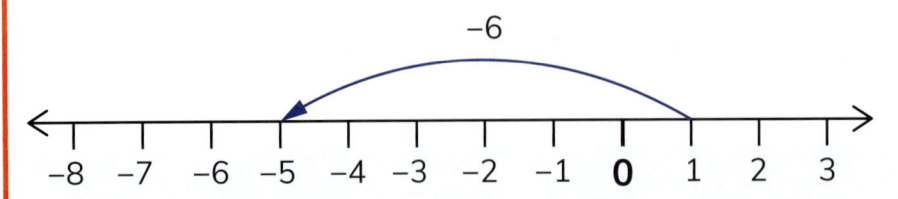
>
> $1 - 6 = -5$
>
> Start at 1 and count back 6.
>
> 6, 1 and −5 are all integers.

Exercise 5.2

This number line shows positive and negative numbers.
You can use it to help you answer the questions in this exercise.

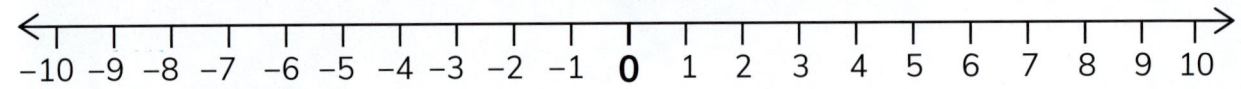

1   Here is part of a number line.

   Find the two missing numbers.

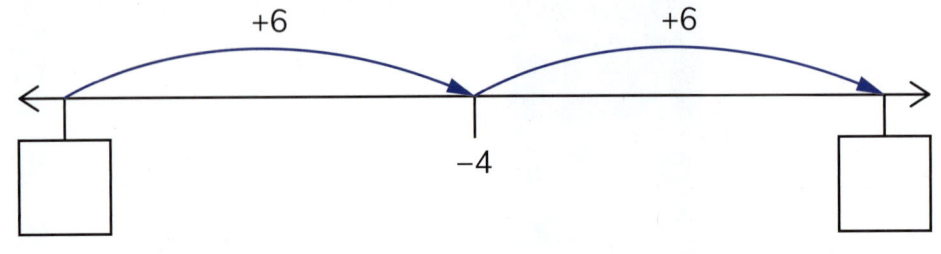

2   a   What is 5 less than 2?   b   What is 4 more than −3?

   c   What is 400 more than −5?   d   What is 30 less than 1?

3   Calculate.

   a   −4 + 2   b   2 − 6   c   −1 + 3

Check your answers to questions 2 and 3 with your partner.
Discuss any questions you did not agree on.

5.2 Addition and subtraction of positive and negative numbers

4 Copy and complete the table.

Temperature now	Rise or fall in temperature	New temperature
2 °C	A fall of 5 degrees	
−3 °C	A rise of 8 degrees	
1 °C	A fall of 5 degrees	
−4 °C	A rise of 2 degrees	
6 °C	A fall of 6 degrees	

5 The thermometers show the temperatures in London and Montreal on the same day.

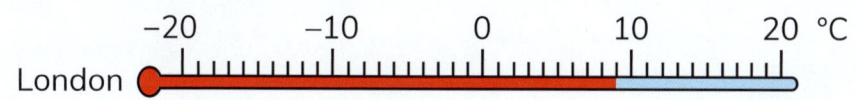

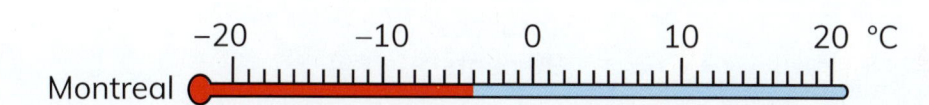

London: (thermometer showing approximately 8 °C)

Montreal: (thermometer showing approximately −8 °C)

a How many degrees colder is it in Montreal than in London?

b On a different day the temperature in London is 4 °C.

Montreal is 16° colder than in London.

What is the temperature in Montreal?

6 Sort these calculations into groups according to their answer.
Label each group.

−4 + 4   −2 − 2   4 + 0   4 − 5
6 − 6   5 − 7   −3 − 1   −4 + 5

7 Calculate.

a 0 − 78   b 45 − 150   c −65 − 35
d −13 + 79   e −8 + 318   f −20 + 370

65

5 Addition and subtraction

Look back over your work. When did you use a number line to help you? Did you draw a line or can you imagine the line in your head? Talk to your partner about the way you use number lines.

Look what I can do!

☐ I can add and subtract positive and negative numbers.

Check your progress

1. The same number goes in both boxes to make this calculation correct. What is the number?

    $0.4 + \boxed{} + \boxed{} = 1$

2. Mia and Aiko buy fruit.

    Mia's fruit: 2 apples and 2 bananas — Total cost 90 cents

    Aiko's fruit: 2 apples and 1 banana — Total cost 65 cents

    How much does one apple cost?

3. A sunflower measures 3.9 metres.
    Ten days later it measures 5.1 metres.
    How much did it grow in that time?

4. Calculate.

    a $-7 + 2$ b $4 - 8$ c $-1 + 204$

5. a What is the sum of 65.98 and 32.75?

    b What is the difference between 54.31 and 46.76?

6 ▶ 3D shapes

Getting started

1   Use the words in the box to name the shape that is made by each net.

cuboid
triangular prism
square-based pyramid
cone
cylinder

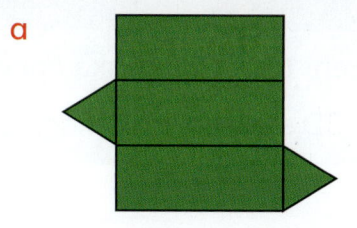

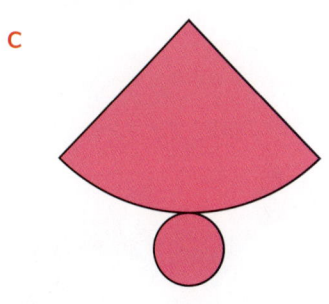

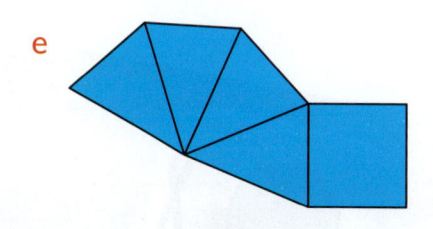

a

b

c

d

e

2   A pentagonal prism has 7 faces.
    What shapes are each of the 7 faces?

3   This is an octagon-based pyramid.
    How many faces does an octagon-based pyramid have?

In this unit you will create 2D drawings of 3D shapes. This is an essential skill in art, design and architecture.

What 2D and 3D shapes can you find in this picture?

6 3D shapes

> 6.1 Nets of cubes and drawing 3D shapes

We are going to ...
- identify and draw the different nets that make open and closed cubes
- identify, describe and draw 3D shapes, including using isometric paper.

Cubes and open cubes are important for design and technology. Where do you see things designed with cubes?

> cube
> open cube

6.1 Nets of cubes and drawing 3D shapes

> **Worked example 1**
>
> Draw this cube on isometric paper. 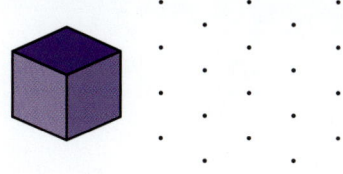
>
> Step 1: 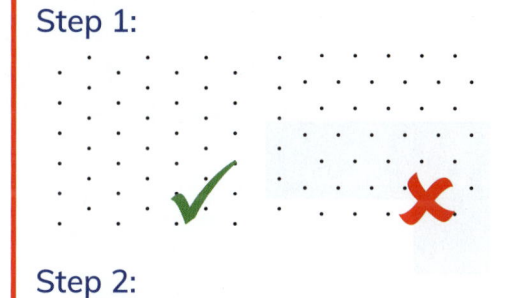
>
> Make sure that your isometric paper is positioned correctly.
>
> Step 2: 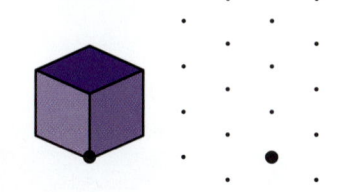
>
> Draw a dot representing one vertex of the cube.
>
> Step 3: 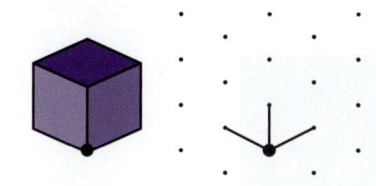
>
> Draw lines that represent the edges of the cube that connect to that vertex.
>
> Step 4: 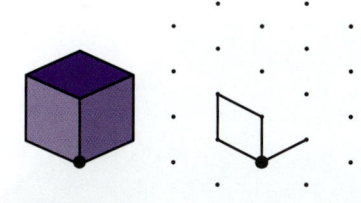
>
> Draw a single face of the cube.
>
> Step 5: 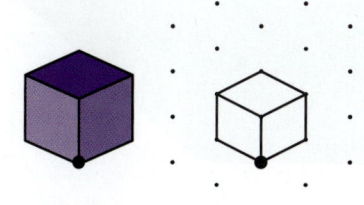
>
> Complete all the other visible faces of the cube.

69

6 3D shapes

Exercise 6.1

1. a How many faces does a cube have?

   b Describe the shape of the faces of a cube.

2. What 3D shape will this net make?

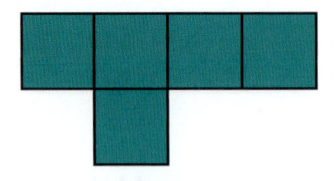

3. Which of these nets will **not** make an open cube?

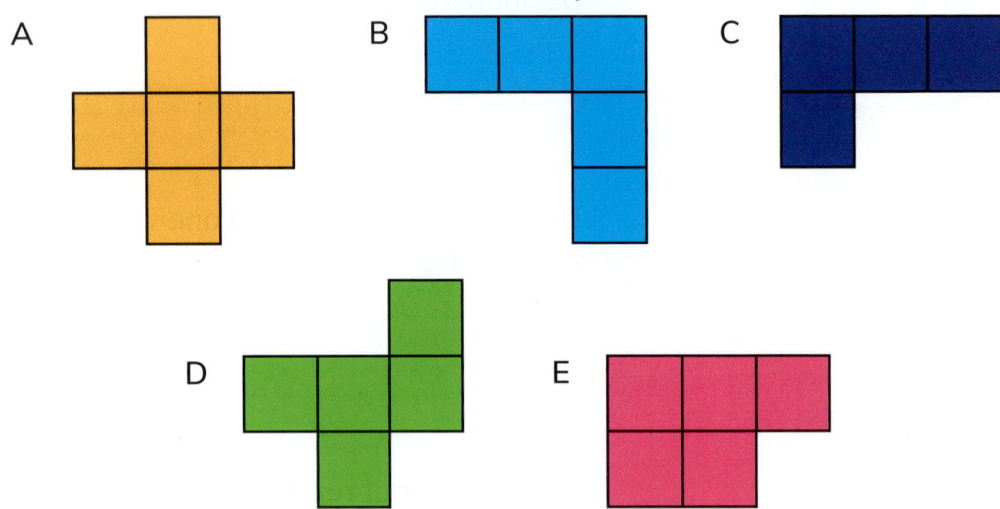

   A   B   C

   D   E

4. Draw a net of a cube.

   Trace this square to use as a template for each face of your cube.

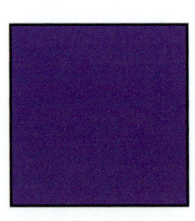

Look at your net of the cube.

How do you know if a net will make a cube?

Do you:
- count the faces?
- visualise the net folding up?
- compare it to nets of cubes you already know?

6.1 Nets of cubes and drawing 3D shapes

5 The diagram shows what Sofia can see when she looks at two different 3D shapes.

Tip

Think about what parts of a 3D shape you can see and what parts you cannot see.

a What two shapes could they be?

b Explain how you know they could be those shapes.

c Sketch each of the shapes in a different orientation. Label each shape with its name.

6 Find a triangular prism. Put the triangular prism on a flat surface and look at it from one position. Draw the triangular prism from your position.

a How many triangles can be seen in your picture?

b How many rectangles can be seen in your picture?

7 Draw these models on isometric paper.

a   b 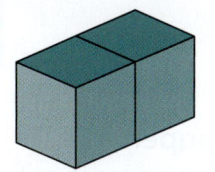   c 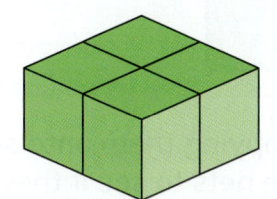   d

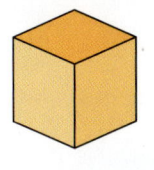

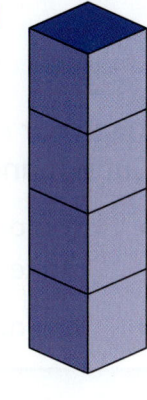

e

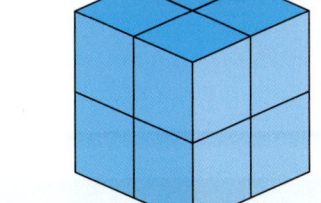

Compare the pictures you have drawn to the pictures shown in the question. How well have you drawn the 3D shapes? What could you do to improve?

71

6 3D shapes

8 Make cuboid **b**, **c**, or **d** shown in question 7 using cubes. Turn the cuboid so that it sits on a different face. Draw the cuboid in its new position on isometric paper.

Think like a mathematician

The net of a cube has been cut into these two pieces.

Imagine the two pieces were stuck together with sticky tape. Draw two sets of nets that can be made by the two pieces stuck together.
One set is the nets that can be folded to make a cube. The other set is the nets that cannot be folded to make a cube.

Example:

Nets that will make a cube with the two pieces

Nets that will not make a cube with the two pieces

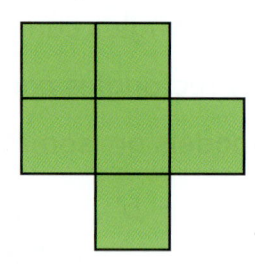

Test your nets by copying them onto squared paper.
Cut out and fold the nets to see if they are in the correct set.

- You are **specialising** when you choose and test a net to see if it will make a cube.
- You are **classifying** when you put each net into a set.

Look what I can do!

☐ I can recognise nets of cubes and open cubes.

☐ I can draw nets of cubes.

☐ I can draw 3D shapes in different orientations.

☐ I can draw 3D shapes on isometric paper.

6.1 Nets of cubes and drawing 3D shapes

Check your progress

1. Draw a net of an open cube.

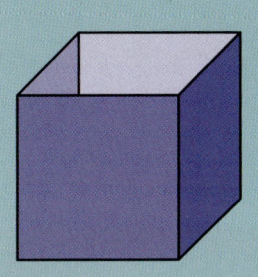

2. Which of these is the net of a cube?

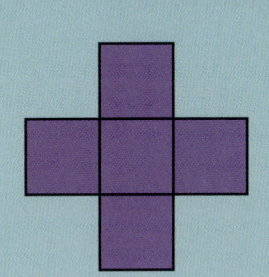

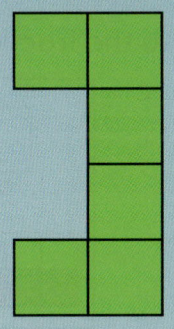

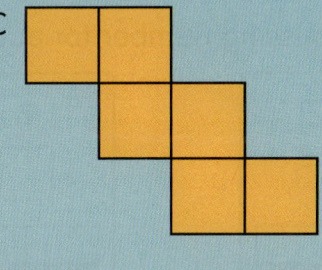

   A   B   C

3. Make a model cuboid that matches this drawing.

   How many cubes did you use?

4. Draw this model on isometric paper.

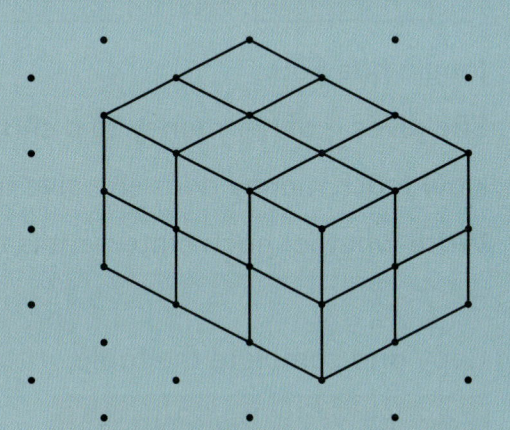

73

7 Fractions, decimals and percentages

Getting started

1. Here are three fraction cards.

   Write the missing number for each card so the fractions are equivalent.

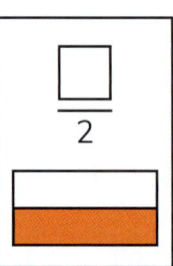

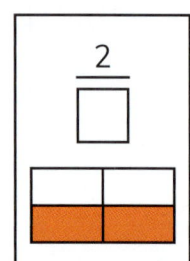

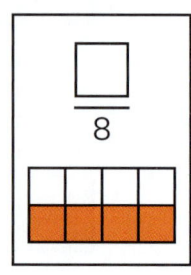

   a) $\frac{\square}{2}$ b) $\frac{2}{\square}$ c) $\frac{\square}{8}$

2. Jamila has $36.

   She gives $\frac{1}{4}$ of her money to a charity.

   How much money does she give to the charity?

3. Write whether each statement is true or false.

   a) $\frac{4}{5} = \frac{4}{5}$ b) $\frac{3}{4} > \frac{17}{20}$ c) $\frac{7}{12} > \frac{3}{4}$ d) $\frac{7}{10} < \frac{4}{5}$

4. Copy and complete the table.

Fraction	Percentage
$\frac{1}{2}$	
$\frac{3}{4}$	

7 Fractions, decimals and percentages

Here are some examples of how we use fractions, decimals and percentages in our everyday lives.

How many more examples can you think of?

Fractions

Decimals

$4.50 $1.50
$3.30 $2.30
$2.00 $5.90

Percentages

75

7 Fractions, decimals and percentages

> 7.1 Understanding fractions

> **We are going to ...**
> - learn to represent a fraction as a division of the numerator by the denominator
> - use a proper fraction as an operator.

You can see fractions being used all around you in everyday life.

½ PRICE SALE NOW ON	A jumper costs $20. How much will it cost in a half-price sale?
(rugby ball)	A rugby game is 80 minutes long. Kick-off is at 15:00. At what time will the half-time break begin?

Key words:
denominator
numerator
operator
proper fraction

Worked example 1

Calculate $\frac{7}{8}$ of 48.

$\frac{1}{8}$ of 48 = 48 ÷ 8   First divide by the denominator to calculate $\frac{1}{8}$.
      = 6

$\frac{7}{8}$ of 48 = 7 × 6   Then multiply by the numerator to calculate $\frac{7}{8}$.
      = 42

Answer: 42

7.1 Understanding fractions

Exercise 7.1

1. Marcus divides a cake into five equal pieces.
   What fraction of the whole cake is each piece?
   Write this fraction as a division.

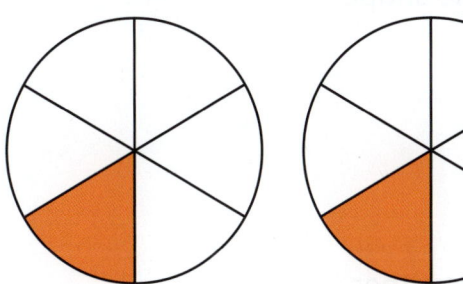

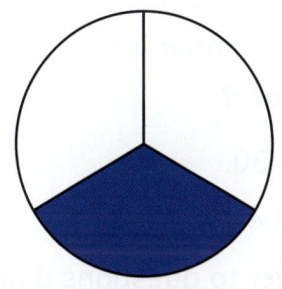

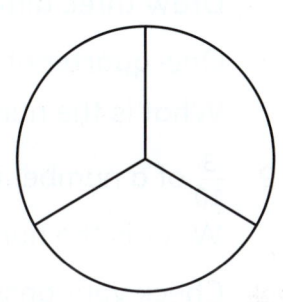

2. Six children share two pizzas equally between them.
   The diagram shows two ways they can do this.

   Draw a diagram to show two different ways eight children can share two pizzas equally.
   How much pizza does each child get?

3. Sofia, Marcus, Zara and Arun share three cakes between them.
   What fraction of a cake does each child get?

4. Calculate.
   a $\frac{2}{3}$ of 15
   b $\frac{3}{4}$ of 24
   c $\frac{3}{5}$ of 60
   d $\frac{6}{7}$ of 84

5. Arun says,

   > To find $\frac{3}{10}$ of 20, I divide by 3 and multiply by 10.

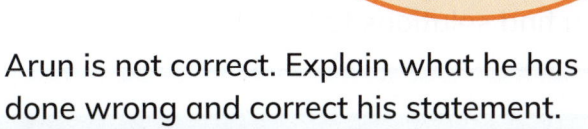

   Arun is not correct. Explain what he has done wrong and correct his statement.

6. Zara has $\frac{1}{5}$ of a bottle of milk.
   There are 100 ml of milk in her bottle.
   How much milk was in the bottle when it was full?

7 Fractions, decimals and percentages

7 These four squares are $\frac{1}{4}$ of a whole shape.

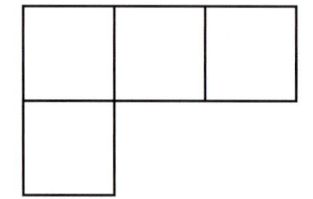

Draw three different shapes that could be the whole shape.

8 One-quarter of a number is 8.
   What is the number?

9 $\frac{3}{10}$ of a number is 30.
   What is the number?

Check your answer to questions 8 and 9 with your partner.

How is question 9 different from 'Find $\frac{3}{10}$ of 30'?
Look carefully at the words in the sentence.
The questions are almost the same, but the answers are different.
This should remind you to read every question carefully.

Think like a mathematician

It is Igor's birthday.

He has 12 cakes.

20 people share the cakes.

Investigate how he could cut the cakes so everyone has an equal share.

You will show you are **specialising** when you find solutions to the problem.

Look what I can do!

☐ I know that a fraction can be represented as a division of the numerator by the denominator.

☐ I can use a proper fraction as an operator.

> 7.2 Percentages, decimals and fractions

> **We are going to ...**
> - write tenths and hundredths, quarters and halves as percentages
> - find percentages of shapes
> - find equivalent proper fractions, decimals and percentages.

In this section you will work with equivalent fractions, decimals and percentages.

$\frac{70}{100}$ $\frac{7}{10}$ 0.7 70%

percentage
per cent

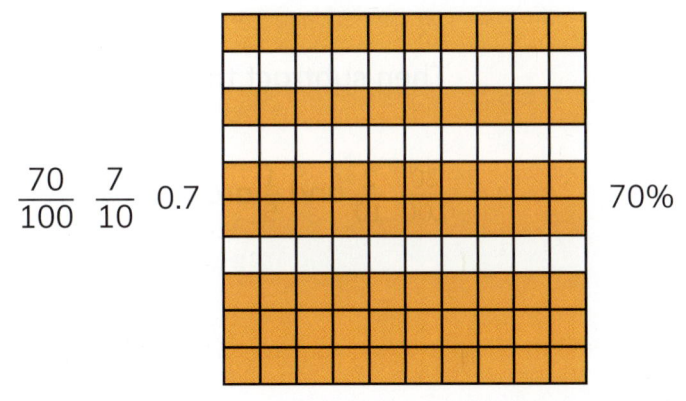

You will find many examples of percentages in everyday life.
Look out for percentage signs next time you go shopping.

7 Fractions, decimals and percentages

> **Worked example 2**
>
> Marcus has a bag of jelly beans.
>
> 30% of the jelly beans are orange, 30% are green, 20% are black and the rest are white.
>
> a   What percentage of the jelly beans are white?
>
> b   What fraction of the jelly beans are black?
>
> ---
>
> a   The percentage that are yellow, green and black is:
>
> 30% + 30% + 20% = 80%
>
> Total percentage is 100.
>
> So, percentage white is:
>
> 100% − 80% = 20%
>
> 20% are white.
>
> b   20% are black.
>
> $20\% = \frac{20}{100}$ or $\frac{2}{10}$ or $\frac{1}{5}$
>
> The whole bag contains 100%
>
> Start by adding up the percentages for yellow, green and black.
>
> Then subtract this from 100.
>
> $\frac{20}{100}$, $\frac{2}{10}$ and $\frac{1}{5}$ are equivalent fractions.
>
> Answer:
>
> a   20%   b $\frac{1}{5}$

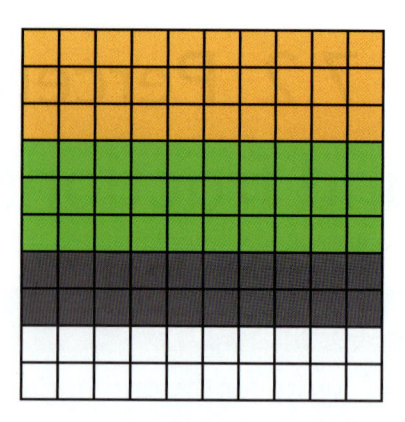

Exercise 7.2

1   Write these fractions as percentages.

   a $\frac{40}{100}$ b $\frac{1}{100}$ c $\frac{1}{10}$

   d $\frac{7}{10}$ e $\frac{1}{4}$ f $\frac{3}{5}$

   Check your answers with your partner.

> **Tip**
>
> Try writing $\frac{3}{5}$ in tenths before changing to a percentage.

7.2 Percentages, decimals and fractions

2   What percentage of each diagram is shaded?

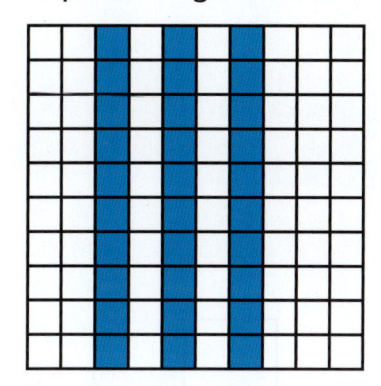

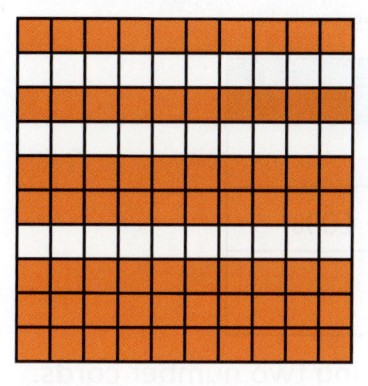

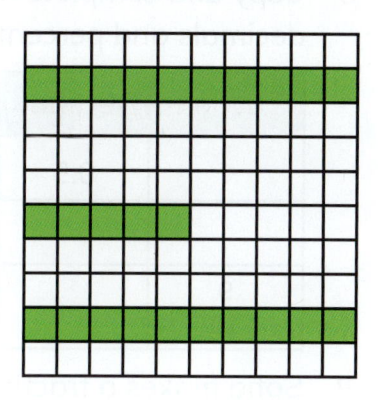

   a   b   c

3   Which is the odd one out in this set of five percentages?
    Explain your answer.

    10%   11%   13%   17%   19%

4   Write the percentage of each shape that is shaded.

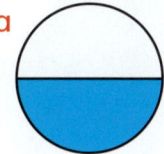

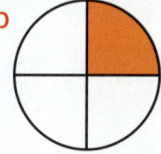

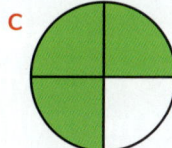

    a   b   c

5   Rajiv draws a pattern of triangles.

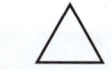

    He colours six triangles.

    a   What fraction of the triangles does he colour?

    b   Write this fraction as a percentage.

6   Find the missing number.

    $\dfrac{5}{\square} = 50\%$

7   Pablo has six cards.

    | 20% | $\dfrac{2}{5}$ | 0.4 | 0.2 | $\dfrac{4}{10}$ | 40% |

    He finds two sets of cards with equivalent values.

    List the two sets.

7 Fractions, decimals and percentages

8 Copy and complete the table to show equivalent fractions, decimals and percentages.

Fraction	Decimal	Percentage
	0.5	
		10%
$\frac{9}{10}$		

9 Sofia makes a fraction using two number cards.

She says, 'My fraction is equivalent to 50%. One of the number cards is 6'.

What fractions could Sofia make?

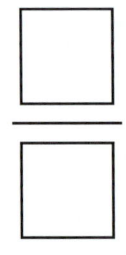

In this exercise, you have answered questions on fractions, decimals and percentages. Think about which questions you found easy and which you found more difficult. How could you improve your work?

Think like a mathematician

Arun has 60 counters.

They are red or yellow or blue or green.

50% of the counters are yellow.

One third of those that are not yellow are red.

0.25 of those that are neither red nor yellow are blue.

The remainder are green.

How many counters are there of each colour?

You will show you are **specialising** when you find solutions to the problem.

7.3 Equivalence and comparison

> **Look what I can do!**
>
> ☐ I can write tenths and hundredths, quarters and halves as percentages.
> ☐ I can find percentages of shapes.
> ☐ I can find equivalent proper fractions, decimals and percentages.

> 7.3 Equivalence and comparison

> **We are going to …**
>
> - find equivalent improper fractions and mixed numbers
> - find equivalent proper fractions, decimals and percentages
> - order and compare proper fractions, decimals and percentages.

In earlier stages, you worked with equivalent proper fractions.

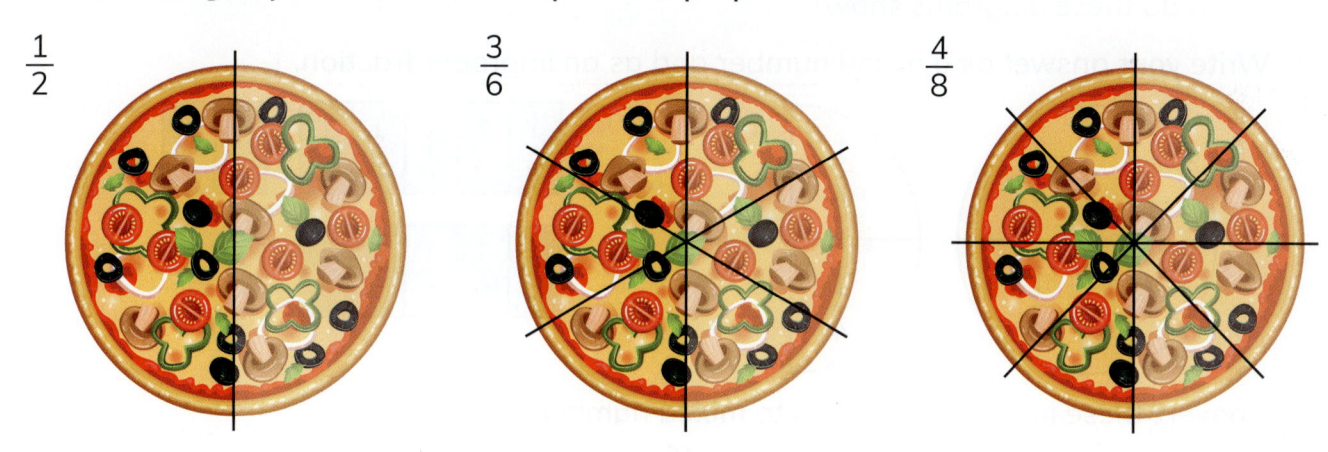

$\frac{1}{2}$ $\frac{3}{6}$ $\frac{4}{8}$

In this section, you will work with equivalent improper fractions and mixed numbers.

You will also order fractions, decimals and percentages.

Can you put these in order starting with the smallest?

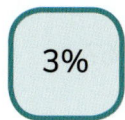

$\frac{1}{10}$ 3%   0.4

improper fraction
mixed number

You need to write them all in the same way to compare them.

83

7 Fractions, decimals and percentages

> **Worked example 3**
>
> Write a mixed number greater than $\frac{12}{4}$ and less than $\frac{14}{4}$.

$\frac{13}{4}$ is between $\frac{12}{4}$ and $\frac{14}{4}$

| $\frac{1}{4}$ | $\frac{1}{4}$ | $\frac{1}{4}$ | $\frac{1}{4}$ | | $\frac{1}{4}$ | $\frac{1}{4}$ | $\frac{1}{4}$ | $\frac{1}{4}$ |

| $\frac{1}{4}$ | $\frac{1}{4}$ | $\frac{1}{4}$ | $\frac{1}{4}$ | | $\frac{1}{4}$ |

It may help you to imagine or draw $\frac{12}{4}$ and $\frac{14}{4}$ on a number line.

Think about how many 'one wholes' you can make from $\frac{13}{4}$.

$\frac{13}{4}$ makes 3 wholes and there is $\frac{1}{4}$ left over.

Answer: $\frac{13}{4} = 3\frac{1}{4}$

Exercise 7.3

1. What do these diagrams show?

   Write your answer as a mixed number and as an improper fraction.

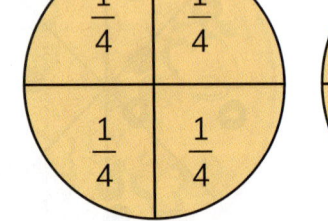

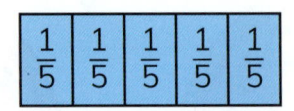

   a [circle divided into quarters and a half-circle showing $\frac{1}{4}$s]

   b [bars showing $\frac{1}{5}$s]

2. Convert these improper fractions to mixed numbers.

   a $\frac{9}{4}$ b $\frac{12}{7}$ c $\frac{16}{3}$ d $\frac{37}{10}$

3. Find the odd one out.

   $1\frac{1}{4}$ $\frac{9}{4}$ $\frac{5}{4}$ $3\frac{1}{4}$ $2\frac{1}{4}$

   Explain your answer.

4. Which of these fractions are equivalent to 40%?

   $\frac{4}{10}$ $\frac{1}{40}$ $\frac{40}{100}$ $\frac{1}{4}$

7.3 Equivalence and comparison

5 Look at the group of fractions, decimals and percentages.

   $\frac{1}{2}$ 20% $\frac{1}{5}$ 0.2

   Find the odd one out.

   Explain why it is the odd one out.

> Questions 3 and 5 involved writing explanations. Did you find that easy or hard? If you found it hard, try explaining your answer to your partner first and then work together to write down your thoughts.

6 Find the missing number.

   a $\frac{9}{\square} = 75\%$ b $\frac{2}{\square} = 25\%$ c $\frac{\square}{50} = 50\%$

7 Order these decimals starting with the smallest.

   2.4   0.3   3.2   2.3   0.2

8 Use one of the symbols <, > or = to complete these statements.

   a $\frac{3}{5}$ ☐ 30%   b 0.4 ☐ $\frac{2}{5}$

   c 25% ☐ $\frac{1}{3}$ d $\frac{1}{4}$ ☐ 0.4

   e 0.7 ☐ $\frac{3}{4}$ f 90% ☐ 0.9

9 Write these fractions, decimals and percentages in order starting with the smallest.

   a 70% $\frac{2}{5}$ 0.1 $\frac{3}{5}$ 50%

   b 0.7 $\frac{4}{5}$ 75% $\frac{3}{5}$ 65%

Look what I can do!

☐ I can find equivalent improper fractions and mixed numbers.

☐ I can find equivalent proper fractions, decimals and percentages.

☐ I can order and compare proper fractions, decimals and percentages.

7 Fractions, decimals and percentages

Check your progress

1. Marcus says, 'I know that one-quarter of a number is 6.

   I can find the number by multiplying 6 by 4.'

   Is Marcus correct?

   Explain your answer.

2. Write $\frac{27}{4}$ as a mixed number.

3. What percentage of each diagram is shaded?

   a 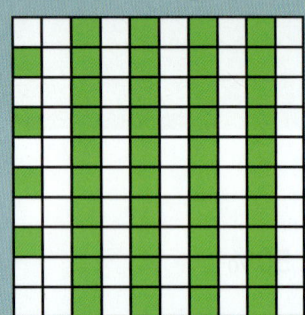   b 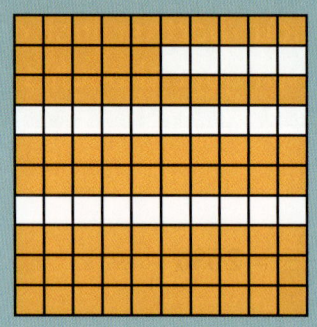   c

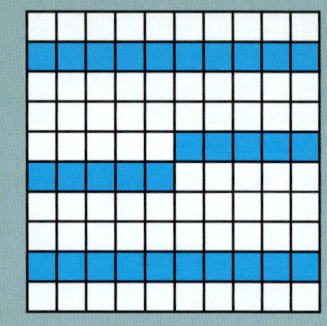

4. Copy and complete this table of equivalent fractions, decimals and percentages.

Fraction	Decimal	Percentage
$\frac{3}{10}$		
		10%
	0.2	
$\frac{23}{100}$		
		25%
	0.7	

5. Write these fractions, decimals and percentages in order starting with the smallest.

   $\frac{3}{4}$ 0.2 $\frac{1}{4}$ 70%   0.3

Project 3

Puzzling percentages

Zara is learning about percentages. She asks 50 children in her year group about their favourite colours.

> 5 out of the 50 children said that their favourite colour was yellow. That's 5% of the children.

What mistake do you think Zara has made?

Can you explain how she could work out what percentage of the children chose yellow as their favourite colour?

Sofia and Marcus are also learning about percentages.
Is Marcus correct? Is Sofia correct? Why or why not?

> I know that 10% is equivalent to one tenth.

> If 10% is equivalent to one tenth then 20% is equivalent to one twentieth.

8 Probability

Getting started

1. There are 6 t-shirts hanging on a washing line. You take one without looking.

   Is each statement true or false?

   a It is certain that you will take a shirt with flowers.

   b There is no chance that you will take a shirt with spots.

   c There is an even chance that you will take a shirt with flowers.

   d There is a poor chance that you will take a shirt with spots.

   e There is a poor chance that you will take a shirt with stripes.

2. An online random generator is used to flip a coin 50 times. Here are the outcomes.

h	h	h	t	t	h	t	t	h	t
t	h	h	h	t	t	t	t	h	h
t	t	t	h	t	h	t	h	h	t
h	h	t	t	h	h	t	t	t	h
h	t	t	t	t	h	t	t	h	h

   Key
   'h' is heads
   't' is tails

   Copy and complete the table to show how many heads and tails there are.

	Tally	Total
Heads		
Tails		

8.1 Likelihood

Probability is about understanding the world and the decisions you make every day. It helps you to decide what risks to take.

These signs all warn you about risks.

How could you find out what the risk is and how likely it is to happen?

> 8.1 Likelihood

We are going to ...

- position the likelihood of events on a likelihood scale
- learn about equally likely events.

Probability can help you make decisions about when to do something.

This astronomer needs a clear sky to look at the stars.

> certain   equally likely   even chance   impossible
> likely   outcome   unlikely

89

8 Probability

She can use a weather forecast to help her decide when to look at the stars.

2100	2200	2300	0000 Wed	0100	0200	0300	0400	0500
15°	14°	13°	12°	11°	10°	10°	9°	9°
0%	1%	3%	3%	3%	3%	2%	2%	3%

When is it likely to be clear?

How likely is it to rain?

What time would be best for studying the stars?

Worked example 1

Draw arrows on the likelihood scale to show the chance of each event happening.

A   Rolling a 5 on a 6-sided dice.

B   Flipping a coin and getting heads.

impossible   unlikely   even chance   likely   certain

There are six possible outcomes on a 6-sided dice.

Only one of the outcomes is 5.

So rolling a 5 is unlikely.

Work out the chance of rolling a 5 on a 6-sided dice.

There are two equally likely possible outcomes when flipping a coin.

One of the outcomes is heads.

Work out the chance of a coin landing on heads.

8.1 Likelihood

> **Continued**
>
> So, there is an even chance that the coin lands on heads.
>
> A   B
> ↓   ↓
> |—————|—————|—————|—————|
> impossible unlikely even chance likely certain
>
> Draw arrows to show the chance of each outcome on the likelihood scale.

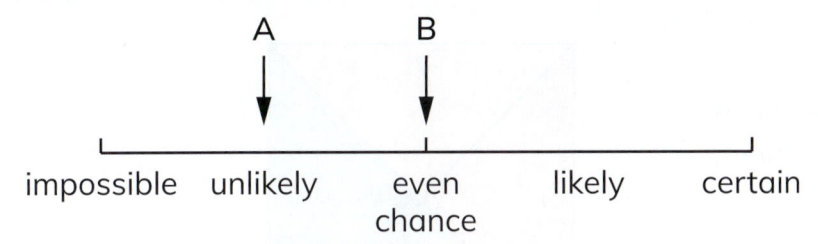

Exercise 8.1

1   Copy this likelihood scale.

   |—————|—————|—————|—————|
   impossible unlikely even chance likely certain

   Draw arrows to show the likelihood of the following events happening.

   a   When you roll a dice you will get a 3.

   b   When you flip a coin it will land on tails.

   c   It will rain today.

   d   Write three statements of your own and add them to the likelihood scale.

> Think about how you used the likelihood scale in question 1. Did you choose events that can be easily positioned on the line?
>
> Do you understand the meaning of all the words on the scale? Ask your teacher if you are not sure about any words.

8 Probability

2 Copy this likelihood scale.

impossible   unlikely   even chance   likely   certain

Look at this spinner.

Mark the likelihood of each of these outcomes on your likelihood scale.

a Scoring an odd number.

b Scoring an even number.

c Scoring less than 5.

d Scoring a number greater than 6.

3 Which two shapes are equally likely to be taken from this bag?

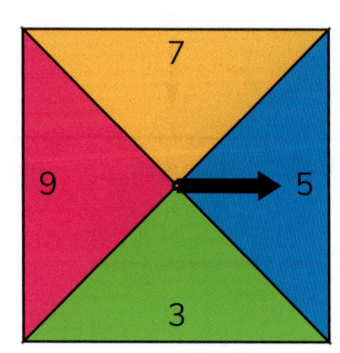

4 Sofia has this bag of letter tiles.

She takes one tile out of the bag at a time.
She writes the letter, then puts the tile back into the bag.

Copy and complete these sentences

a There are ____ letter tiles.

b ____ of the tiles are the letter E.

c The chance of taking a letter E is unlikely / even chance / certain.

d It is equally likely that Sofia will take letter ____ or letter ____ .

e Letter ____ is the most likely to be taken.

5 Write two sentences of your own about the likelihood of Sofia taking different tiles from the bag in question 4.

8.1 Likelihood

Think like a mathematician

Sarah and Lou are playing a game with two coins.

They flip both the coins.

Sarah scores one point if the coins both land heads up.

Lou scores one point if one coin is heads and one is tails.

No points are scored if the coins both land tails up.

Do you think that Sarah and Lou are equally likely to win?

Draw a table to record the coin flips.

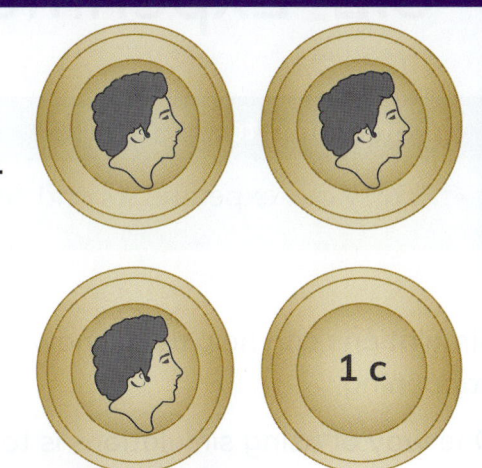

	Tally	Total
Sarah's score		
Lou's score		

Flip two coins 50 times and record your results.

Do the results of the coin flips suggest that Sarah and Lou are equally likely to win the game?

Talk to your partner and teacher about your results and write down your thoughts about the game using the language of chance.

- You are **conjecturing** when you form an idea about whether Sarah and Lou are equally likely to win.

- You are **convincing** when you explain your results to your partner and teacher.

Read your sentences about chance to your partner.

Does your partner use the language of chance correctly to show that they understand it?

Talk to your partner about your answers.

Look what I can do!

☐ I can position the likelihood of events on a likelihood scale.

☐ I can say if two events are equally likely.

8 Probability

8.2 Experiments and simulations

We are going to ...

- carry out experiments and simulations to investigate probability.

Simulations can help us to know the likelihood of an outcome happening.

One way of using simulations is to program a computer to use data from previous outcomes to work out what would happen if something was done thousands of times.

These simulations can try to predict things like whether a goal is likely to be scored from different positions on a football pitch.

> simulation

8.2 Experiments and simulations

> **Worked example 2**
>
> Marcus wants to simulate whether a cat will have male or female kittens.
>
> He flips a coin. If the coin lands heads up it represents a male kitten. If the coin lands tails up it represents a female kitten.
>
> Is this an appropriate simulation?

The kittens could be male or female.

- The likelihood of a kitten being male is even chance.
- The likelihood of a kitten being female is even chance.
- It is equally likely that the kittens will be male or female.

Describe the likelihood of the real outcomes.

The coin could land on heads or tails.

- The likelihood of the coin landing on heads is even chance.
- The likelihood of the coin landing on tails is even chance.
- It is equally likely that the coin will land heads or tails.

Describe the likelihood of the outcomes on the flipped coin.

Answer: Yes, a flipped coin is an appropriate way to simulate whether the kittens will be male or female because the outcomes are equally likely and the coin has two equally likely outcomes.

8 Probability

Exercise 8.2

1. You are going to do an experiment to investigate the likelihood of different outcomes when you roll two dice and find the difference between the two numbers.

    a What different outcomes can you get if you roll two dice and find the difference between the two numbers?

    b Do you think that all the outcomes are equally likely?

    c Copy the table and complete the first column.

The difference between the two numbers	Tally	Frequency

    d Roll two dice 30 times and record the results in your table.

    e Draw a bar chart to show your results.

    A bar chart showing the frequency of different outcomes when I throw two dice and find the difference between the two numbers

    Frequency

    The difference between the two numbers

    f Do your results suggest that the outcomes are all equally likely?

    g What could you do to check?

2 There are five shapes in a bag.

Arun took a shape out of the bag, looked at it and put it back into the bag. He did this eight times. These are the shapes he saw.

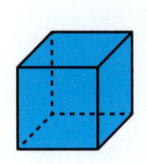

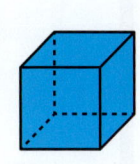

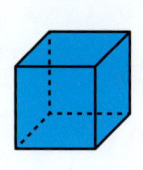

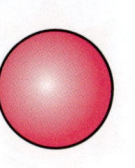

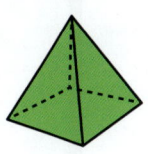

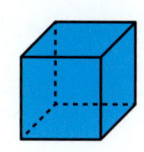

cube, cube, sphere, cylinder, cube, sphere, square-based pyramid, cube

a Write true or false for each statement.
   i   There was at least one sphere in the bag.
   ii There was definitely not a triangular prism in the bag.
   iii There might be more than one cube in the bag.
   iv There is definitely only one cylinder in the bag.
b Sketch the five shapes that you predict might be in the bag.
c Explain why you chose those five shapes for your prediction.
d What could you do to improve your prediction without looking into the bag?

3 Rachel programmed a spreadsheet to simulate 50 coin flips. The spreadsheet creates random numbers from 1 to 3.

Rachel says, 'The odd numbers represent coin flips that land on heads.

The even numbers represent coin flips that land on tails.'

Rachel's spreadsheet list looks like this:

3	1	2	2	2	2	3	3	1	3
1	3	2	3	1	3	3	3	1	2
3	1	3	2	3	2	3	3	2	1
3	1	2	3	2	1	1	3	1	2
1	3	2	3	2	2	3	2	2	1

a How many even numbers are in Rachel's list?
b How many odd numbers are in Rachel's list?
c Explain what is wrong with Rachel's simulation.
d Suggest a better way to simulate the coin flips using random numbers.

8 Probability

4 The weather forecast says that there is an even chance of rain for the next 7 days.

Even chance

Sofia made a simulation of the weather using a dice.

Numbers 1, 2 and 3 are rainy days.

Numbers 4, 5 and 6 are dry days.

Sofia rolled the dice 7 times to see what might happen. These are her results.

Day 1	Day 2	Day 3	Day 4	Day 5	Day 6	Day 7
5	4	2	1	5	3	4

a How many rainy days are there in Sofia's simulation?

b How many dry days are there in Sofia's simulation?

c Draw your own table and carry out your own simulation of the weather using Sofia's rules.

d How many rainy days are there in your simulation?

e How many dry days are there in your simulation?

Think about how you are using the dice to simulate the chance of rain. The likelihood of rain is an even chance. What other things could you use to simulate an even chance?

8.2 Experiments and simulations

> **Think like a mathematician**
>
> Use computer software to generate 100 random numbers from 1 to 20.
>
> a   How many times does the number 1 appear in the list?
>
> b   How many numbers in the list are greater than 10?
>
> c   How many numbers in the list are less than 6?
>
> d   Generate another set of 100 random numbers from 1 to 20. Answer questions **a**, **b** and **c** using the 100 new numbers.
>
> e   Zara says that the numbers 1 to 20 are all equally likely so each number will appear the same number of times in the list.
>
> Explain why Zara is wrong.
>
> Look at your partner's explanation.
>
> Did they write about the results of their simulation?
>
> Did they write about how the more random numbers the computer produces, the closer the results will be to showing that the numbers are all equally likely?
>
> - You are **characterising** when you describe the sets of random numbers.
> - You are **convincing** when you explain why Zara is wrong.

Look what I can do!

☐ I can carry out experiments and simulations to investigate probability.

Check your progress

1   Draw a likelihood scale.

   impossible   unlikely   even chance   likely   certain

Look at the picture of the pile of sweets. Draw arrows on the scale to show the likelihood of the following events happening.

a   Taking a strawberry sweet.

b   Taking an orange sweet.

c   Taking a banana sweet.

8 Probability

Continued

2. Compare and describe the likelihood of taking a lemon sweet and the likelihood of taking a lime sweet from the pile in question 1.

3. Marcus has collected seeds to grow. He knows that 1 seed out of every 4 does not grow.

   He uses this spinner to simulate how many of his seeds will grow into plants. He spins it once for each seed he has.

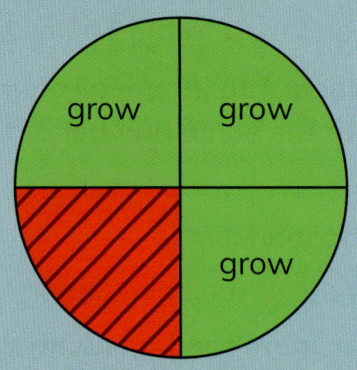

   These are Marcus's results:

   | green | green | red | red | green | green | green | green |
   | red | green | red | red | red | green | green | green |

   a How many seeds does Marcus have?

   b How many of Marcus's seeds grow in the simulation?

   c How many of Marcus's seeds do not grow in the simulation?

   d Use probability language to describe the likelihood that a seed will grow.

9 Addition and subtraction of fractions

Getting started

1 What is $\frac{3}{4} + \frac{1}{4}$?

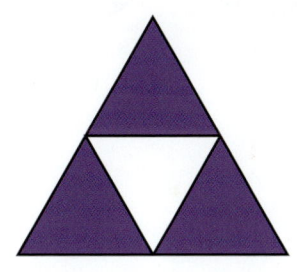

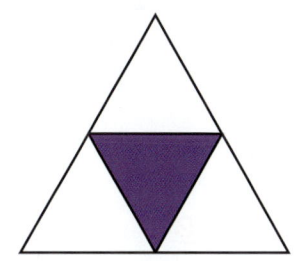

2 What number do you add to $\frac{2}{3}$ to equal $\frac{7}{3}$?

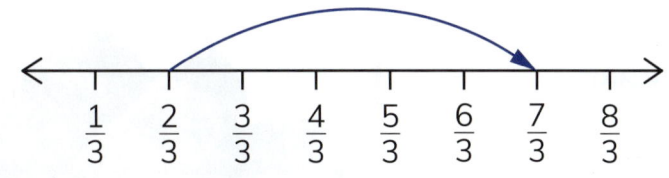

3 Find the missing fractions.

   a $\frac{11}{4} - \frac{5}{4} = \frac{\Box}{\Box}$

   b $\frac{\Box}{\Box} + \frac{3}{4} = \frac{13}{4}$

4 Yuri adds two fractions. This is his working.

   $\frac{8}{7} + \frac{2}{7} = \frac{10}{14}$

   Yuri is not correct. Explain what he has done wrong. What is the correct answer?

9 Addition and subtraction of fractions

Here are some examples of using fractions.

Adding and subtracting fractions:

$$\frac{2}{3} - \frac{1}{3} = \frac{1}{3}$$

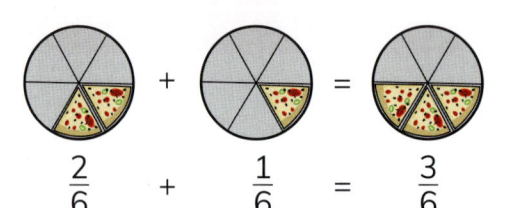

$$\frac{2}{6} + \frac{1}{6} = \frac{3}{6}$$

A banana bread recipe:

Banana bread

3 bananas

$\frac{1}{3}$ cup melted butter

$\frac{2}{3}$ cup sugar

1 egg

$\frac{3}{4}$ teaspoon vanilla

$\frac{1}{2}$ teaspoon baking soda

$1\frac{1}{2}$ cups flour

Serves 10 people.

The Ancient Egyptians used unit fractions.

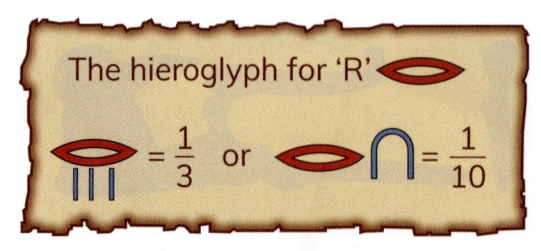

The hieroglyph for 'R'

$= \frac{1}{3}$ or $= \frac{1}{10}$

Discuss with your partner when you see or use fractions.

> 9.1 Addition and subtraction of fractions

> **We are going to ...**
> - add and subtract two fractions with the same denominator
> - add and subtract two fractions with denominators that are multiples of each other.

This cake is cut into nine equal pieces.

Imagine Andri, Ben, Carlos and George each have a piece of cake.

To find out how much cake has been eaten, we add fractions:

$$\frac{1}{9} + \frac{1}{9} + \frac{1}{9} + \frac{1}{9} = \frac{4}{9}$$

To find out how much cake is left, we subtract the total from one whole:

$$1 - \frac{4}{9} = \frac{5}{9}$$

In this section, you will learn to add and subtract fractions that do not have the same denominator.

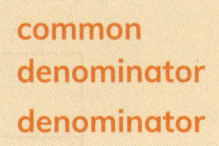

> common denominator
> denominator

Worked example 1

Use the fraction wall to calculate $\frac{2}{3} + \frac{5}{6}$.

1					
$\frac{1}{3}$		$\frac{1}{3}$		$\frac{1}{3}$	
$\frac{1}{6}$	$\frac{1}{6}$	$\frac{1}{6}$	$\frac{1}{6}$	$\frac{1}{6}$	$\frac{1}{6}$

9 Addition and subtraction of fractions

> **Continued**
>
> $\frac{2}{3} + \frac{5}{6}$
>
> $= \frac{4}{6} + \frac{5}{6}$
>
> $= \frac{9}{6}$
>
> Answer: $\frac{2}{3} + \frac{5}{6} = \frac{9}{6}$
>
> Write both fractions as sixths. (6 is the denominator of $\frac{5}{6}$ and the common denominator of both fractions.)
>
> Add the numerators to give 9 sixths.

Exercise 9.1

1 Use the fraction wall to calculate.

a $\frac{2}{3} - \frac{1}{6}$

b $\frac{1}{6} + \frac{1}{3}$

2 The fractions $\frac{9}{10}$ and $\frac{1}{5}$ have been shaded on the fraction wall.

Calculate.

a $\frac{9}{10} - \frac{1}{5}$

b $\frac{7}{10} - \frac{2}{5}$

You can draw diagrams to help you answer the remaining questions in this exercise.

9.1 Addition and subtraction of fractions

3 Calculate.

a $\dfrac{2}{5} + \dfrac{7}{10}$
b $\dfrac{2}{3} + \dfrac{5}{9}$
c $\dfrac{11}{12} + \dfrac{3}{4}$

d $\dfrac{2}{3} + \dfrac{7}{12}$
e $\dfrac{3}{5} + \dfrac{7}{20}$
f $\dfrac{3}{4} + \dfrac{3}{8}$

4 Calculate.

a $\dfrac{5}{6} - \dfrac{1}{3}$
b $\dfrac{7}{15} - \dfrac{1}{5}$
c $\dfrac{7}{12} - \dfrac{1}{4}$

d $\dfrac{7}{8} - \dfrac{3}{4}$
e $\dfrac{13}{15} - \dfrac{2}{5}$
f $\dfrac{11}{12} - \dfrac{1}{3}$

Check your answers to questions 3 and 4 with your partner.

Compare the methods you used to answer the questions.

5 Eva and Mia share a pizza with their dad.

Eva eats $\dfrac{1}{3}$ of the pizza.

Mia eats $\dfrac{1}{6}$ of the pizza.

What fraction of the pizza do they leave for their dad?

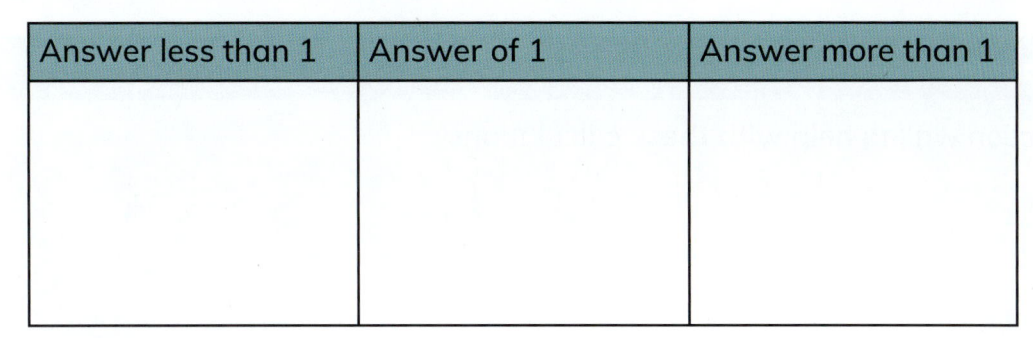

6 Copy the table and write the letters of the calculations in the correct columns.

a $\dfrac{1}{10} + \dfrac{2}{5}$
b $\dfrac{4}{5} + \dfrac{3}{10}$
c $\dfrac{3}{5} + \dfrac{2}{5}$
d $\dfrac{7}{10} + \dfrac{1}{5}$

Answer less than 1	Answer of 1	Answer more than 1

7 Write the missing numbers.

a $\dfrac{\square}{20} + \dfrac{7}{10} = \dfrac{17}{20}$
b $\dfrac{1}{3} + \dfrac{\square}{12} = \dfrac{9}{12}$
c $\dfrac{\square}{16} + \dfrac{3}{4} = \dfrac{19}{16}$

Look back over the questions in this exercise.

Which methods did you find easiest to use?

What can you do to improve your work?

9 Addition and subtraction of fractions

> **Think like a mathematician**
>
> The Ancient Egyptians only used unit fractions, for example $\frac{1}{2}$ or $\frac{1}{3}$.
>
> Find a way to write $\frac{3}{8}$ as the sum of two unit fractions.
>
> Now find $\frac{6}{10}$ and $\frac{7}{18}$ as the sum of two unit fractions.
>
> **Challenge:** Try to write $\frac{7}{10}$ as the sum of two unit fractions.
>
> Find other examples of a fraction of your choice written as the sum of two unit fractions.
>
> You will show you are **specialising** when you find solutions to the problem.
>
> > **Tip**
> >
> > Remember $\frac{1}{4} = \frac{2}{8}$

Look what I can do!

☐ I can add and subtract two fractions with the same denominator.

☐ I can add and subtract two fractions with denominators that are multiples of each other.

Check your progress

1 Use the fraction wall to help with these calculations.

   a $\frac{3}{4} + \frac{1}{8}$ b $\frac{1}{2} - \frac{1}{8}$ c $\frac{1}{8} + \frac{1}{4}$ d $\frac{5}{8} - \frac{1}{4}$

1							
$\frac{1}{2}$				$\frac{1}{2}$			
$\frac{1}{4}$		$\frac{1}{4}$		$\frac{1}{4}$		$\frac{1}{4}$	
$\frac{1}{8}$	$\frac{1}{8}$	$\frac{1}{8}$	$\frac{1}{8}$	$\frac{1}{8}$	$\frac{1}{8}$	$\frac{1}{8}$	$\frac{1}{8}$

9.1 Addition and subtraction of fractions

Continued

2 Copy this diagram and use it to help you calculate $\frac{1}{4} - \frac{1}{12}$.

   Find the answer.

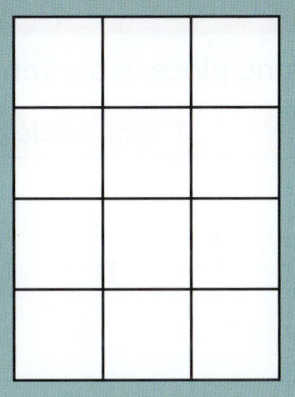

3 Copy this number line and use it to show $\frac{1}{2} - \frac{3}{8}$. Find the answer.

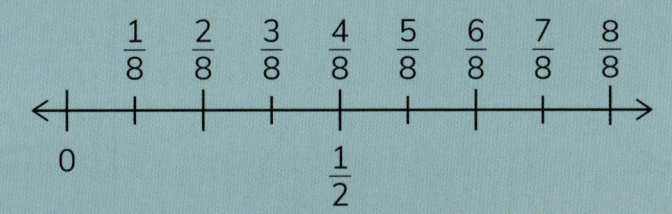

4 This is a diagram of a vegetable garden.

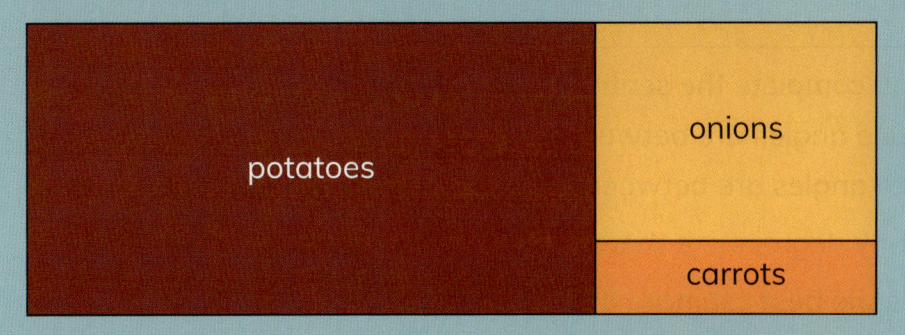

   $\frac{2}{3}$ of the garden is planted with potatoes.

   $\frac{3}{12}$ of the garden is planted with onions.

   What fraction of the garden is planted with carrots?

10 Angles

Getting started

1 Which angles are in the wrong place in the table?

Acute angles	Right angles	Obtuse angles
A, B, C	D, E, F	G, H, I

2 Copy and complete the sentences.

   a Obtuse angles are between 90 degrees and ____ degrees.

   b Acute angles are between ____ degrees and 90 degrees.

3 How many degrees are there in four right angles?

4 Which is the best estimate for the size of this angle?

   A 80 degrees

   B 130 degrees

   C 170 degrees

   D 90 degrees

Angles are used for estimating and comparing sizes.

Look at the picture.

How much of the cake has gone?

What is the angle of the remaining cake?

Can you estimate the sizes of the pieces using angles?

Are the angles obtuse, acute or right angles?

> 10.1 Angles

> **We are going to …**
> - use the degrees symbol when recording angles
> - learn about reflex angles
> - estimate angles
> - learn about the sum of angles on a straight line.

It is important to be able to talk about shapes, parts of shapes and amounts of turn accurately.

What words do you already know about angles?

Choose one of these shapes to describe to your partner.

Can they work out which shape you are describing?

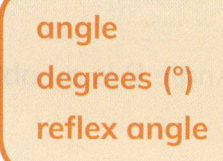

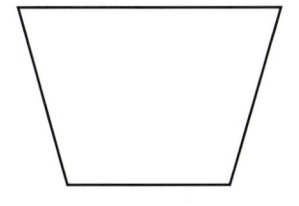

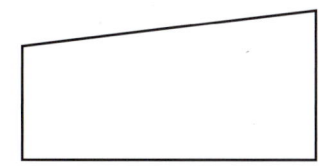

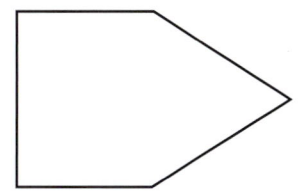

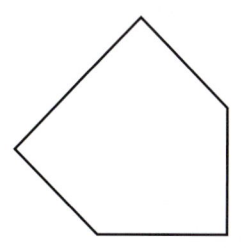

> angle
> degrees (°)
> reflex angle

In this section you will learn a new word for describing a type of angle.

109

10 Angles

> **Worked example 1**

Which of these is a reflex angle?

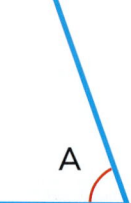

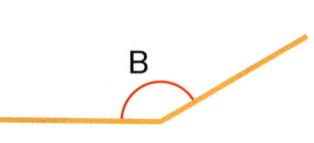

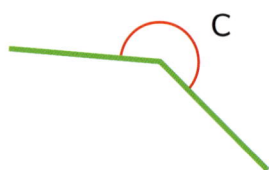

Angle A is smaller than a right angle, which is 90 degrees.

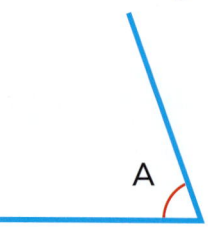

Reflex angles are greater than 180 degrees, so angle A is not a reflex angle.

Angle A is an acute angle.

Angle B is greater than 90 degrees but smaller than 180 degrees.

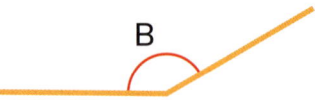

Reflex angles are greater than 180 degrees, so angle B is not a reflex angle.

Angle B is an obtuse angle.

Angle C is greater than 180 degrees and smaller than 360 degrees.

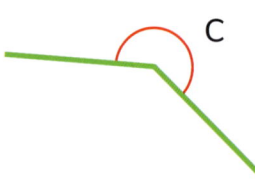

Answer: Angle C is a reflex angle.

10.1 Angles

Exercise 10.1

1 Which of these are reflex angles?

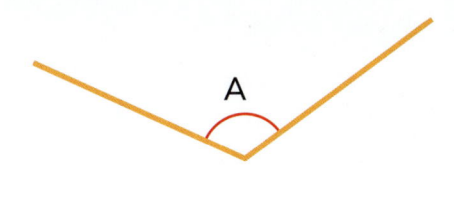

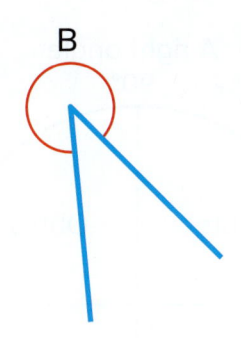

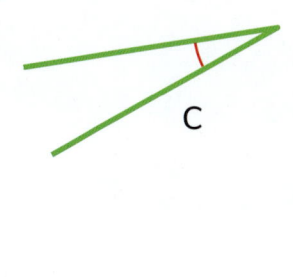

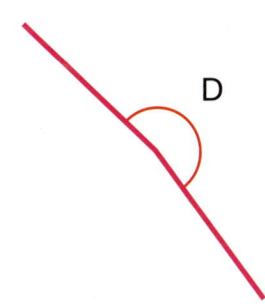

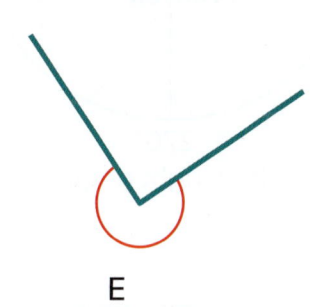

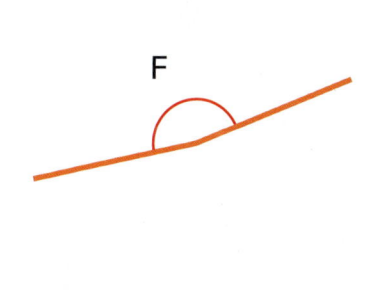

A   B   C

D   E   F

2 Write 'acute', 'obtuse', 'reflex' or 'right angle' for each angle.

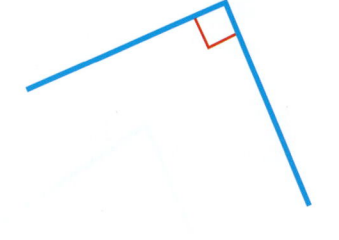

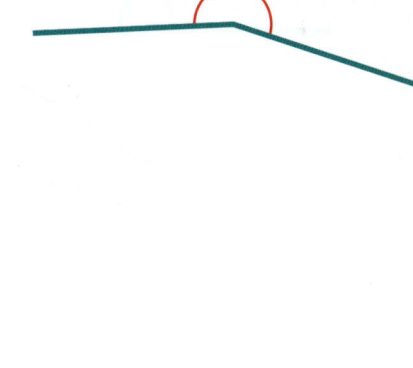

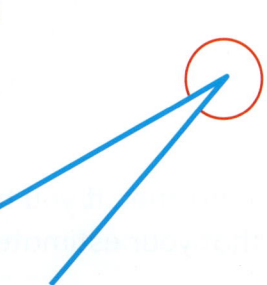

a   b   c

d   e

3 Compare the angles in question 2.
   a Which is the smallest angle?
   b Which is the largest angle?
   c Write the letters of the angles in order from smallest to largest angle.

111

10 Angles

4 Use this diagram to help you to estimate the size of each angle. You could use tracing paper and a ruler to help you compare the angles to the angles on the diagram.

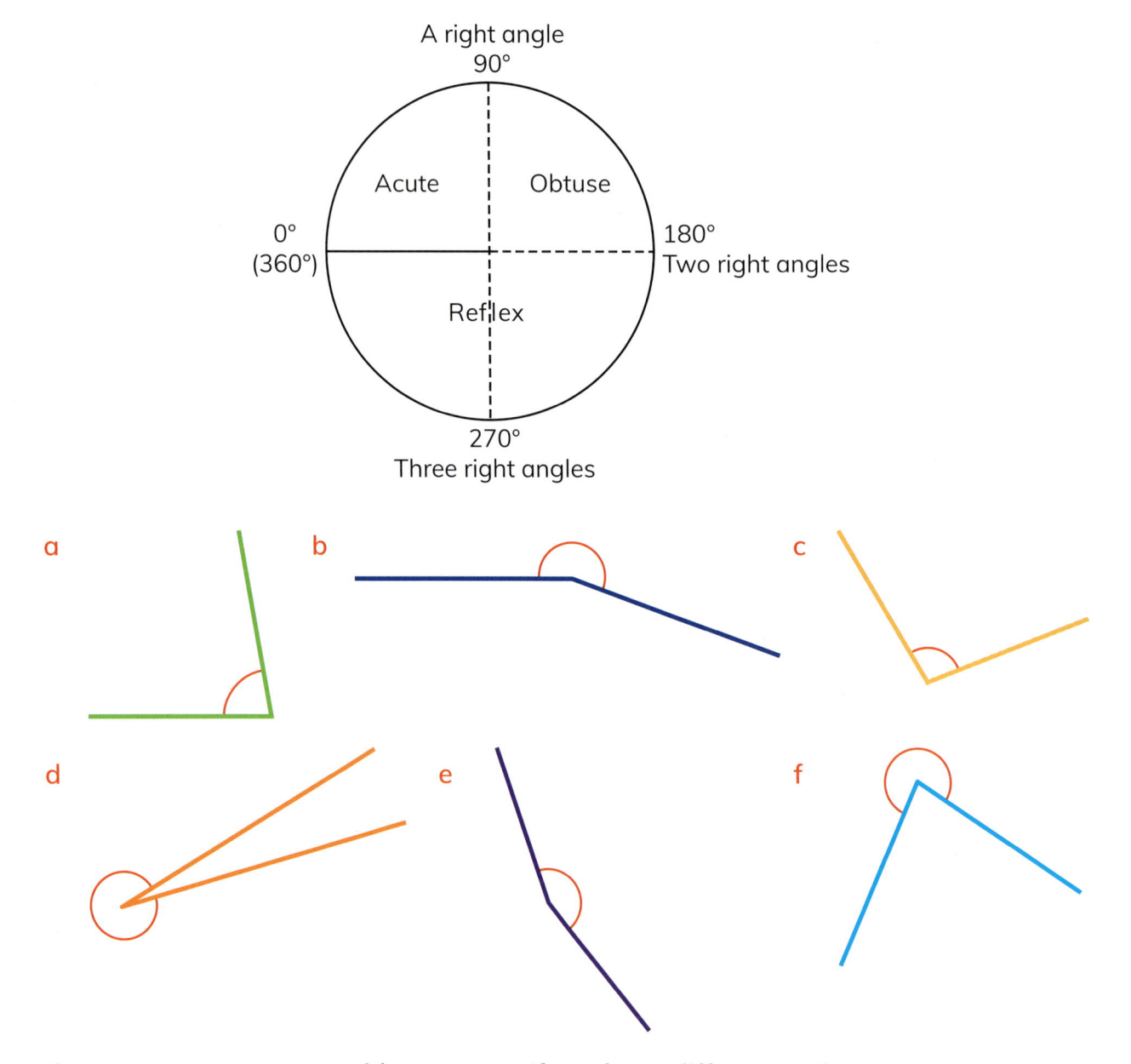

A right angle
90°

Acute | Obtuse

0° (360°) | 180° Two right angles

Reflex

270°
Three right angles

a   b   c

d   e   f

Compare your answers with a partner. If you have different estimates, try to convince your partner that your estimate is best.

When you compare your estimates to your partner's, did you find that they were higher, lower or about the same?

What can you do to improve how well you estimate angles?

10.1 Angles

5   The angles on a straight line add up to 180°.

Jaret makes a plan to show the angle of the spotlights for the school play.

Work out the missing angles a, b, c and d.

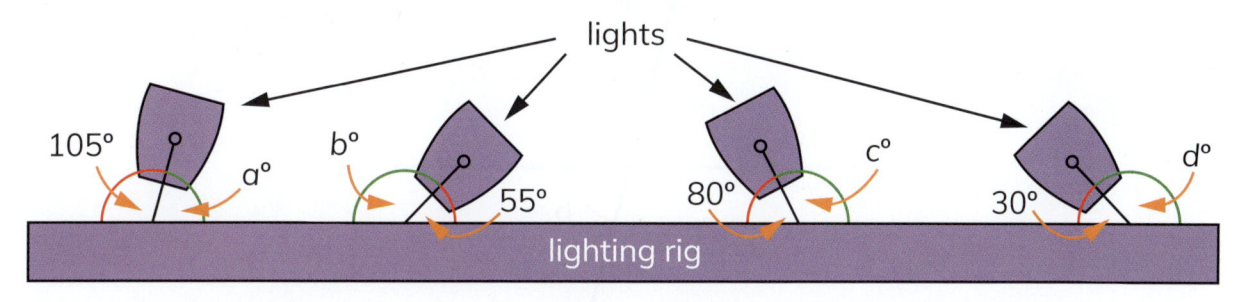

6   These semi-circular pies have been cut into pieces.

What are the missing angles?

Write your answers using the ° symbol.

a

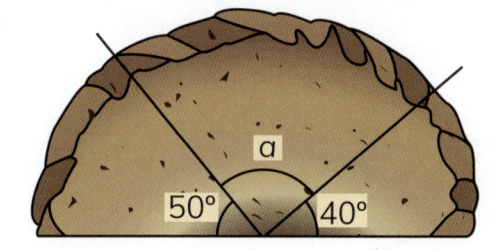

b

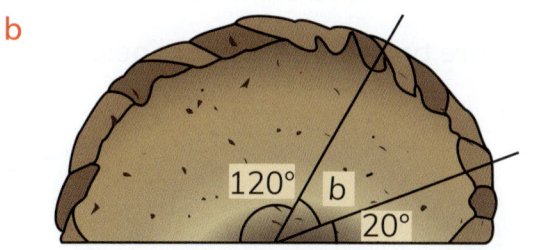

c

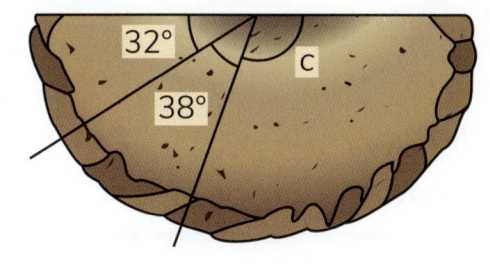

d

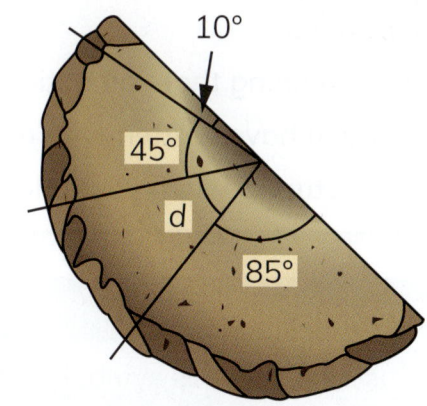

113

10 Angles

Think like a mathematician

Here are two straight lines.

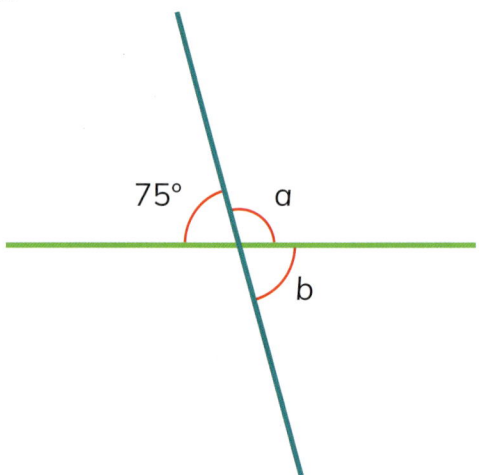

[Diagram showing a horizontal green line crossed by a diagonal line, with 75° on the upper left, angle a on the upper right, and angle b on the lower right.]

Work out angle a.
Angle a is on a straight line with angle b. Work out angle b.

Here are two more straight lines.

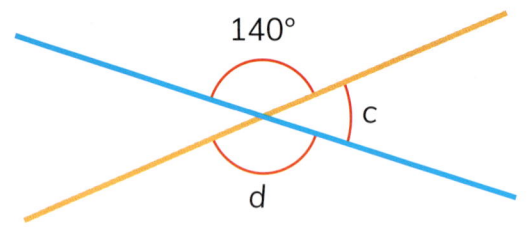

[Diagram showing two crossing lines with 140° at the top, angle c on the right, and angle d at the bottom.]

Work out angle c.
Work out angle d.
Write down anything that you notice about the angles.
Share what you have written with a partner and discuss.
You are **conjecturing** when you reflect on what you notice about the angles.

Look what I can do!

☐ I can use the degrees symbol to record angles.
☐ I can recognise acute, obtuse and reflex angles.
☐ I can estimate angles.
☐ I can calculate angles on a straight line.

10.1 Angles

Check your progress

1 Write 'acute', 'obtuse', 'reflex' or 'right angle' for each angle.

   a   b    c

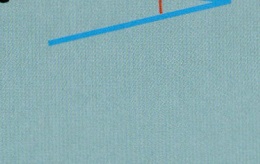

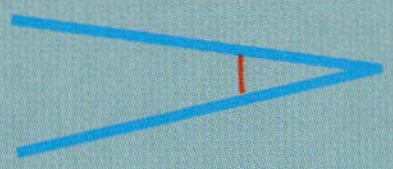

   d 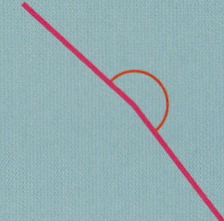   e 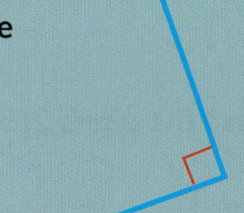   f

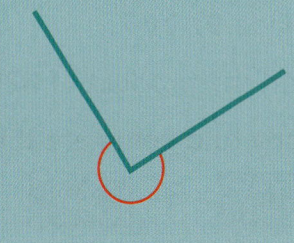

2 Estimate the size of each angle.

   a   b    c

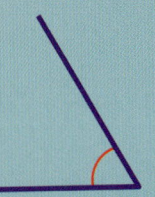

3 Copy and complete this sentence.

   The angles on a straight line add up to _____°

4 What are the missing angles on these straight lines?

   a 100°, a

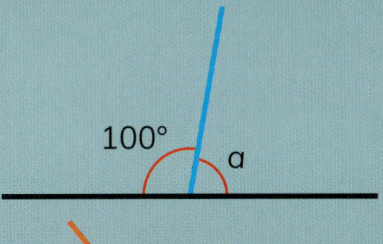

   b 20°, b

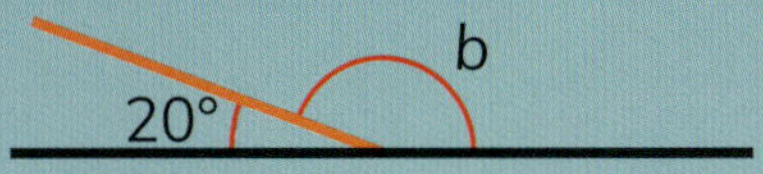

   c 50°, c, 30°

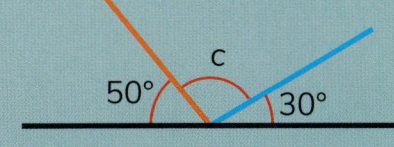

   d 25°, 30°, d, 75°

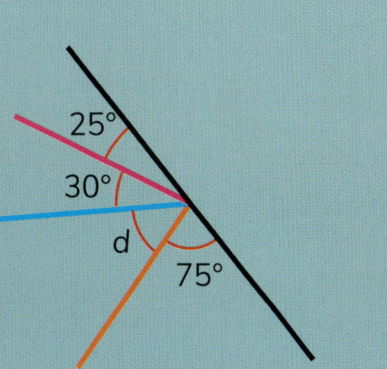

11 Multiplication and division

Getting started

1. Divide 97 by 7.
2. Find the product of 829 and 9.
3. Copy and complete this calculation. Use the digits 2, 5 and 7.

   ▢▢ × 3 = ▢▢

4. Find the odd one out. Explain your answer.

   24 ÷ 3   40 ÷ 5   72 ÷ 9
         54 ÷ 6   64 ÷ 8

5. Using all the digits 0, 1, 3 and 5 each time, find:

   a the largest even number divisible by 5.

   b the smallest number, greater than 1000, that is divisible by 25.

11 Multiplication and division

Look at the picture of a warehouse full of food. The food is packed carefully to make the best use of the space available.

Soup is packed in trays.

There are 24 tins in one tray.

Six trays are packed in one box.

A supermarket orders 7 boxes of tomato soup, 5 boxes of chicken soup and 4 boxes of vegetable soup.

How can you work out the number of tins of soup the supermarket orders?

Work with your partner to find the answer. You may need to use a calculator.

This unit is all about multiplication and division.

Can you think of other situations where you need to multiply or divide?

11 Multiplication and division

> 11.1 Multiplication

We are going to ...
- estimate the size of an answer before calculating it
- multiply whole numbers by 1-digit and 2-digit whole numbers.

We all learn how to multiply in school and many people use multiplication in their jobs.

Imagine you work in a large warehouse. Your job is to load boxes onto a lorry. You have to work out what the mass of all the boxes will be.

The calculations involve multiplication.

product

Mass calculation

Mass of box = ▢

Number of boxes = ▢

Total mass = mass of box × number of boxes

= ▢

11.1 Multiplication

> **Worked example 1**
>
> Calculate 56 × 27
>
> Estimate: 60 × 30 = 1800   Always start with an estimate.
>
> | | | 5 | 6 |
> |---|---|---|---|
> | | × | 2 | 7 |
> | 1 | 1 | 2 | 0 |
> | | | 3 | 9 | 2 |
> | 1 | 5 | 1 | 2 |
> | | 1 | | |
>
> Multiply 56 by 20
>
> Multiply 56 by 7
>
> Add the two answers together.
>
> You can also do the multiplications the other way around and multiply 56 by 7 first and then 56 by 20.
>
> Answer: 56 × 27 = 1512

Exercise 11.1

1   Calculate. Remember to estimate the size of your answer before you calculate it.

   a 400 × 9   b 60 × 8   c 300 × 7
   d 90 × 6   e 900 × 4   f 40 × 8

2   Which calculations give the answer 2400?

   30 × 80   60 × 40   30 × 60   120 × 20   80 × 20

3   A hummingbird beats its wings about 75 times each second.

   About how many times does it beat its wings in a minute?

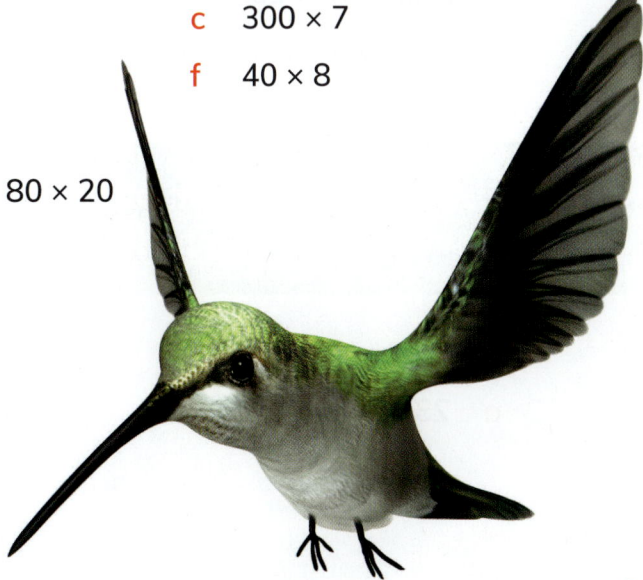

11 Multiplication and division

4. Find the product of 31 and 76.

5. Sofia is calculating 299 × 60.

   She estimates that the answer is 180 000.

   Has she made a good estimate?

   Explain your answer.

6. A storeroom has boxes stacked in 12 rows.

   Each row contains 96 boxes.

   How many boxes are there altogether?

7. Arun multiplied 24 by 12.

   Here is his working.

			2	4
×			1	2
	2	4	0	0
			4	8
	2	4	4	8

   What error has Arun made? How should he improve his work?

8. Calculate 37 × 25.

   Discuss with your partner the most efficient way of working out the answer.

Think about the different methods of multiplying.
Which method do you prefer. Why?

9. Calculate.

   a 236 × 48   b 179 × 57   c 987 × 36

11.2 Division

Think like a mathematician

You need four cards.

| 3 | 5 | 4 | 6 |

Arrange the cards as a multiplication calculation.

Investigate different answers. Try to find as many as you can and then find the largest and smallest answers.

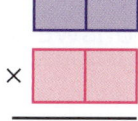

You will show you are **specialising** when you find solutions to the problem.

Look what I can do!

☐ I can estimate the size of an answer before calculating it.

☐ I can multiply whole numbers by 1-digit and 2-digit whole numbers.

> 11.2 Division

We are going to ...

- estimate the size of an answer before calculating it
- divide whole numbers by 1-digit whole numbers.

Imagine you are in a music group. You might be the singer, a guitarist or the drummer. When you play a song, it is divided into different parts so each person has their own job to do.

When a music group is paid to perform, the money is divided between the members of the group.

Imagine an extra person joins the group.

Will each member of the group get more or less money when it is divided out?

decompose
denominator
divisor
inverse operations
numerator

121

11 Multiplication and division

> **Worked example 2**
>
> Calculate 736 ÷ 8

Estimate:	Start with an estimate.
800 ÷ 8 = 100 and 720 ÷ 8 = 90	
So the answer is between 90 and 100.	Using the estimate 720 ÷ 8 = 90 we can work out that 730 ÷ 8 = 90 with 10 left over.

```
      9
  ┌─────────
8 │ 7   3 ¹6
```

Record 9 tens on the answer line.

Carry 1 ten to the ones column.

```
      9   2
  ┌─────────
8 │ 7   3 ¹6
```

16 ÷ 8 = 2

Record 2 ones on the answer line.

There is no remainder.

Answer: 736 ÷ 8 = 92

Exercise 11.2

1   Calculate. Remember to estimate the size of your answer before you calculate it.

   a   456 ÷ 8   b   868 ÷ 7   c   333 ÷ 9

2   Zina's book has 238 pages.

   She reads 7 pages each day.

   How long does it take Zina to read the book?

3   Calculate, writing the remainder as the number left over.

   a   638 ÷ 5

   b   423 ÷ 4

   c   326 ÷ 8

11.2 Division

4 Classify the calculations into these groups:
- answer less than 10
- answer between 10 and 20
- answer more than 20

| 86 ÷ 3 | 88 ÷ 9 | 91 ÷ 9 | 94 ÷ 8 | 96 ÷ 6 | 98 ÷ 4 |

Discuss your answer with your partner.

How did you do the calculation? How did you decide which category to put it in? How did you record your answer?

5 Calculate, writing the remainder as a fraction.

a 97 ÷ 5   b 86 ÷ 4   c 99 ÷ 7

Check your answers with your partner.

6 Find the missing numbers.

a ☐ ÷ 4 = 23   b ☐ × 4 = 96   c 88 ÷ ☐ = 22

7 Find the missing digit.

☐ 9 2 ÷ 7 = 5 6

Think about the questions in this exercise. Which question was the most difficult? If you were asked to do a similar question, what would you do differently?

Think like a mathematician

Use only the digits 4, 5 and 9 to find numbers to make this number sentence correct.

Use each digit only once.

☐☐☐ ÷ 9 = a whole number

Find as many different answers as you can.

What is the largest answer you can get?

You will show you are **specialising** when you find solutions to the problem.

123

11 Multiplication and division

> **Look what I can do!**
> ☐ I can estimate the size of an answer before calculating it.
> ☐ I can divide whole numbers by 1-digit whole numbers.

> 11.3 Tests of divisibility

We are going to ...

- learn and use tests of divisibility for 4 and 8.

You can use divisibility tests to find out if one number can be divided by another number without having to do the division calculation.

A number that is only divisible by 1 and the number itself is called a prime number. You learnt about prime numbers in Unit 3.

What is the name for numbers that are not prime numbers?

> divisible
> divisibility test
> Venn diagram

Prime numbers

1	2	3	4	5	6	7	8	9	10
11	12	13	14	15	16	17	18	19	20
21	22	23	24	25	26	27	28	29	30
31	32	33	34	35	36	37	38	39	40
41	42	43	44	45	46	47	48	49	50
51	52	53	54	55	56	57	58	59	60
61	62	63	64	65	66	67	68	69	70
71	72	73	74	75	76	77	78	79	80
81	82	83	84	85	86	87	88	89	90
91	92	93	94	95	96	97	98	99	100

_____ numbers

1	2	3	4	5	6	7	8	9	10
11	12	13	14	15	16	17	18	19	20
21	22	23	24	25	26	27	28	29	30
31	32	33	34	35	36	37	38	39	40
41	42	43	44	45	46	47	48	49	50
51	52	53	54	55	56	57	58	59	60
61	62	63	64	65	66	67	68	69	70
71	72	73	74	75	76	77	78	79	80
81	82	83	84	85	86	87	88	89	90
91	92	93	94	95	96	97	98	99	100

11.3 Tests of divisibility

> **Worked example 3**
>
> Use the numbers 48, 49, 50, 51 and 52 **once** to make these number sentences correct.
>
> ▭ is a multiple of 3.
> ▭ is divisible by 4.
> ▭ is divisible by 5.
> ▭ is divisible by 8.
> ▭ is a square number.
>
> **Answer:**
>
> | | |
> |---|---|
> | 51 is a multiple of 3. | 48 and 51 are multiples of 3. |
> | 52 is divisible by 4. | 48 and 52 are divisible by 4. |
> | 50 is divisible by 5. | Only 50 is divisible by 5. |
> | 48 is divisible by 8. | Only 48 is divisible by 8. |
> | 49 is a square number. | Only 49 is a square number. |
>
> Place 48, 49 and 50 in the last three boxes, then decide how to fill in the first two boxes.

Exercise 11.3

1 Look at this set of numbers.

   a Write the numbers that are divisible by 2.

   b Write the numbers that are divisible by 4.

   366   422   14 432   790 124   234 444   555   146   160

2 Write down the numbers from this list that are divisible by 4.

   113   342   632   218   488   784

   How do you know they are divisible by 4?

   Check your answer with your partner.

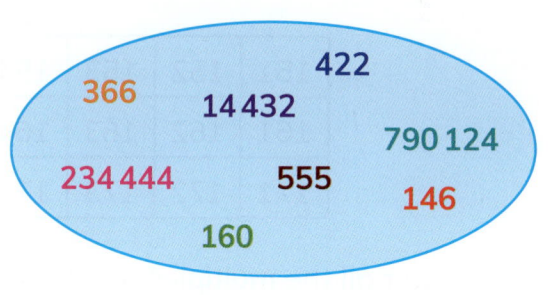

125

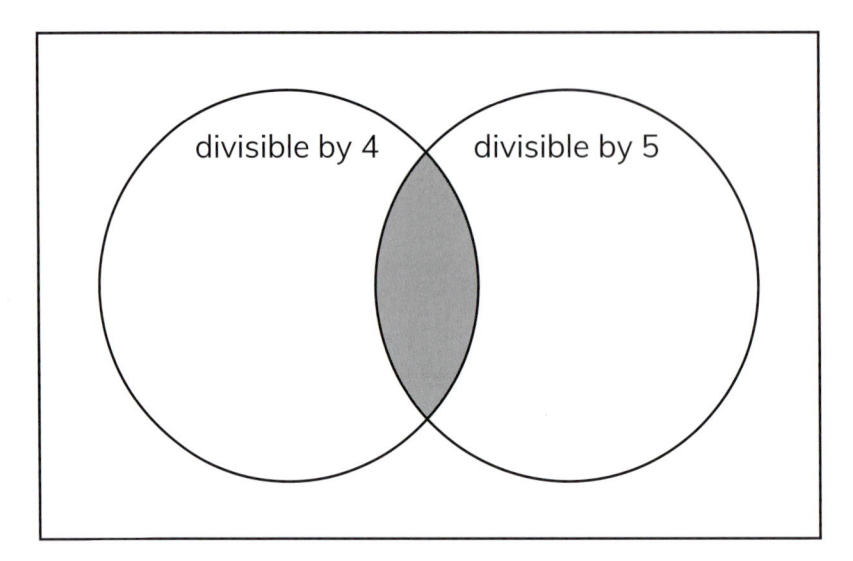

11 Multiplication and division

3 Copy and complete the Venn diagram to show where these numbers go.

304   25   203   400   205   52   502

Venn diagram with two overlapping circles labelled "divisible by 4" and "divisible by 5"; the intersection is shaded grey.

The grey area is the intersection of two sets.
What can you say about the numbers in the intersection?

4 This sequence shows multiples of 4.

4, 8, 12, 16, 20, ...

Will 114 be in the sequence?

Explain how you know.

5 Here is a number grid.

151	152	153	154	155	156	157	158	159	160
161	162	163	164	165	166	167	168	169	170
171	172	173	174	175	176	177	178	179	180

a List all the multiples of 4 that are on the grid.

b List all the multiples of 8 that are on the grid.

6 Copy and complete the Venn diagram to show where these numbers go.

24 302   56 824   987 204   43 200

12 404   969 696

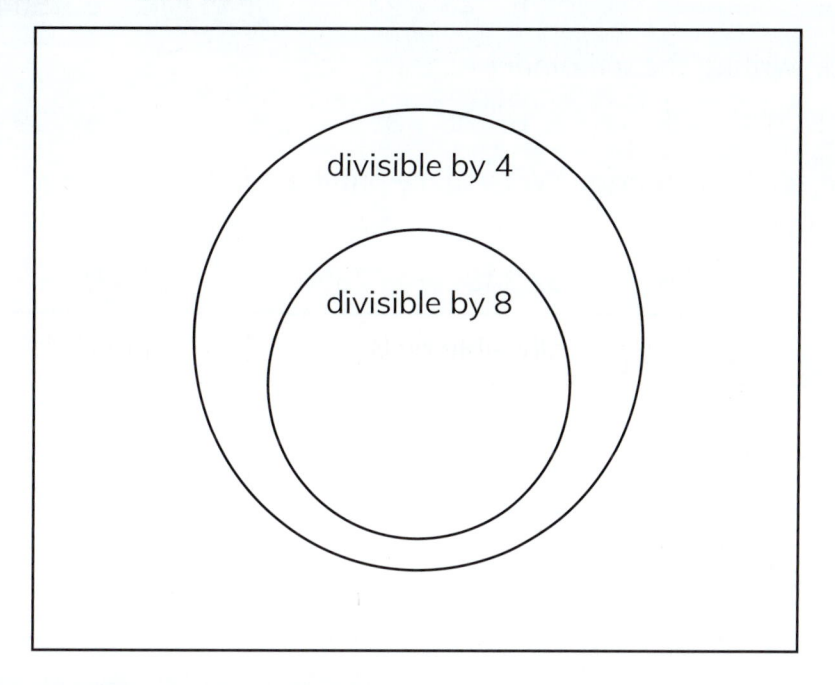

(Venn diagram: outer rectangle, with a circle labelled "divisible by 4" containing an inner circle labelled "divisible by 8")

7 a Write down a number which is divisible by 4 and 8.

  b Write down a number which is divisible by 4 and 5.

  c Write down a number that is divisible by 2, 4, 5, 10 and 100.

> Think about how you answered part c. If a number is divisible by 100, it is also divisible by all the factors of 100. 2, 4, 5 and 10 are all factors of 100.

Think like a mathematician

Is it always, sometimes or never true that the sum of four even numbers is divisible by 8?

You will show you are **convincing** when you explain your findings.

Look what I can do!

☐ I know and can use tests of divisibility for 4 and 8.

11 Multiplication and division

Check your progress

1. Calculate.

   a 408 × 7   b 46 × 24   c 504 ÷ 9

2. Calculate, writing the remainder as a fraction.

   a 98 ÷ 5   b 86 ÷ 3   c 89 ÷ 7

3. Copy the sorting diagram. Write these numbers in the correct place on the diagram.

   23 456   51 466   62 848   76 343   97 631

	divisible by 8	not divisible by 8
even		
odd		

4. Here are four digit cards.

   0   1   3   5

   Use these cards to complete the calculation.

   Each card can be used once only.

   ☐☐ × ☐☐ = 450

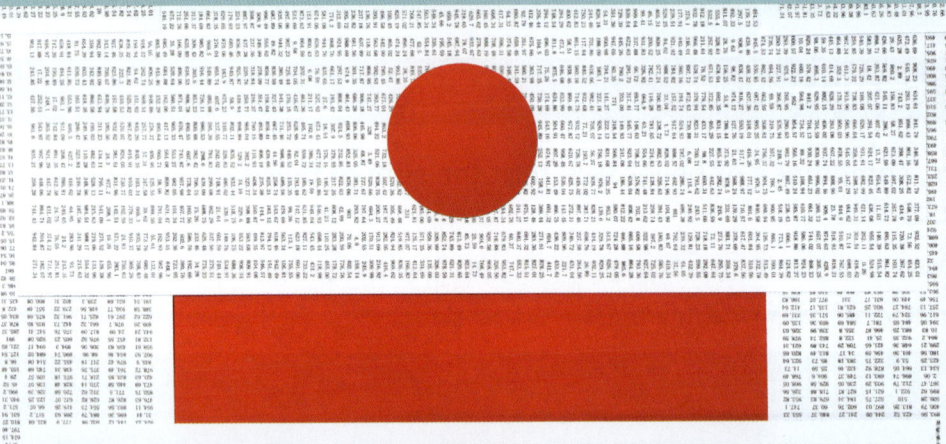

12 Data

Getting started

1   Look at these two bar charts.

Bar chart showing the heights of children in Hexagon Class

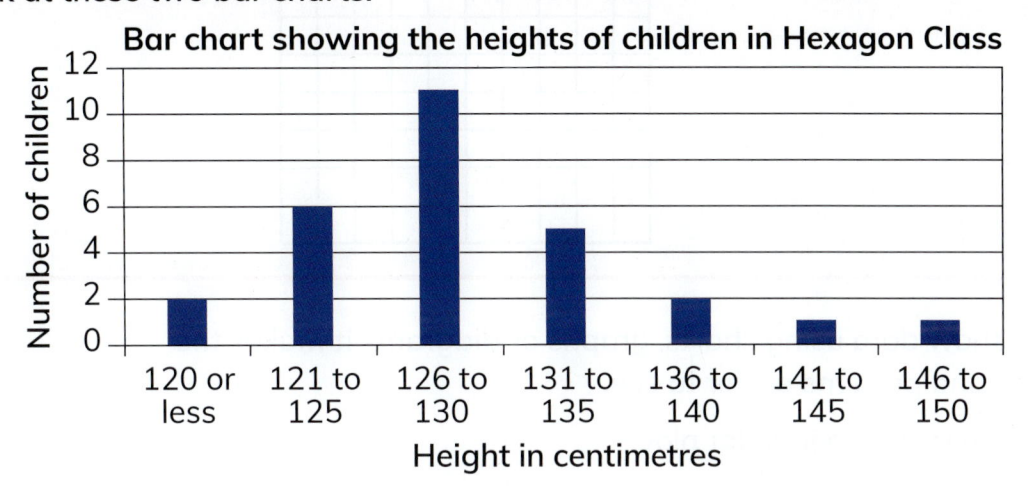

(Number of children vs Height in centimetres)
- 120 or less: 2
- 121 to 125: 6
- 126 to 130: 11
- 131 to 135: 5
- 136 to 140: 2
- 141 to 145: 1
- 146 to 150: 1

Bar chart showing the heights of children in Pentagon Class

(Number of children vs Height in centimetres)
- 120 or less: 0
- 121 to 125: 3
- 126 to 130: 4
- 131 to 135: 6
- 136 to 140: 10
- 141 to 145: 5
- 146 to 150: 2

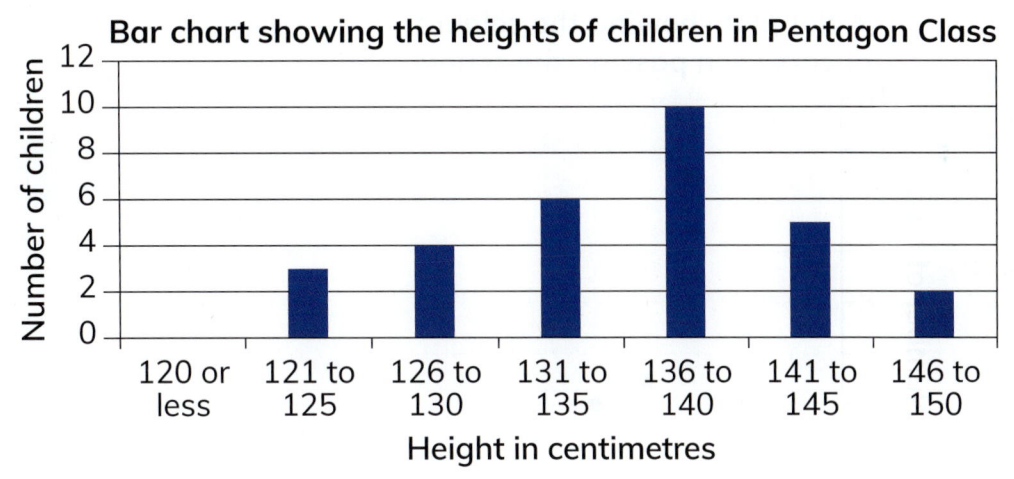

   a   How many children in Hexagon Class are 126 to 130 cm tall?

   b   How many children in Pentagon Class are 141 cm or taller?

   c   How many children are there in total in each class?

   d   More children in Pentagon Class are 136 cm or taller than in Hexagon Class. Write about why there might be a difference in the height of children in Pentagon Class and Hexagon Class.

129

12 Data

> **Continued**
>
> 2 What percentage of this diagram is shaded?

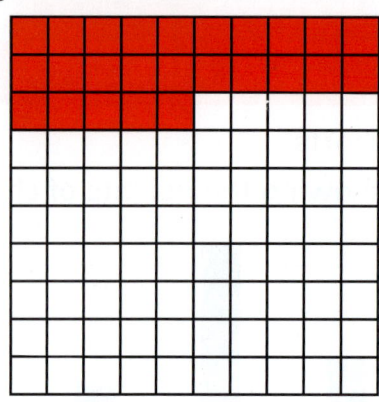

When you show data using charts, graphs or diagrams it makes the information and patterns easier to see.

The data here is shown in a dot plot.

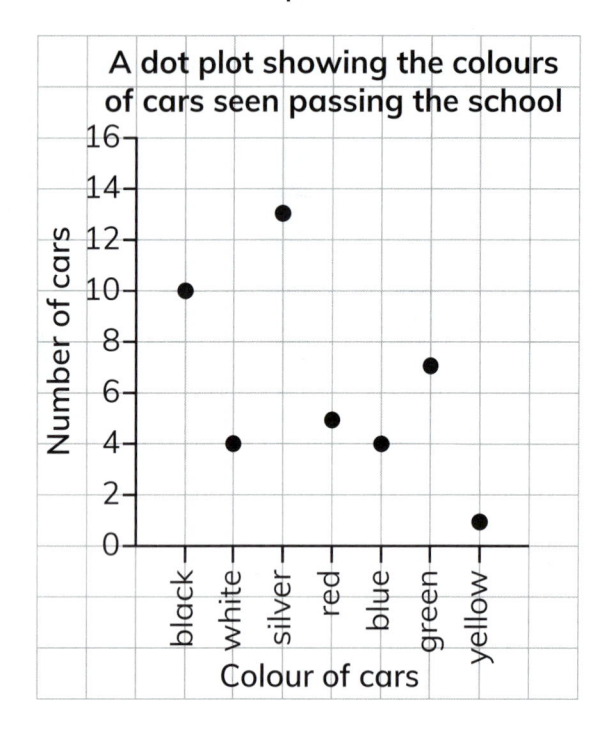

A dot plot showing the colours of cars seen passing the school

(Number of cars vs Colour of cars: black 10, white 4, silver 13, red 5, blue 4, green 7, yellow 1)

What information can you work out from the dot plot?

There are lots of different ways to display data.

How many other ways can you think of to display data?

In this unit you will learn more about some of the ways to display data so that you can explain information clearly.

> 12.1 Representing and interpreting data

We are going to ...

- investigate questions by collecting data
- represent data using tables, bar charts, dot plots and waffle diagrams
- find patterns in data to answer statistical questions.

In this section you will explore and use a variety of ways to display data so you can understand and interpret it more easily. You will use bar charts, dot plots and waffle diagrams to help you compare different sets of data.

bar chart   data
dot plot
statistical question
waffle diagram

What might you use each of these items for when you are collecting and representing data?

12 Data

> **Worked example 1**
>
> Some people were asked to choose their favourite flower. These are the results.
>
> Rose: 10   Lily: 5   Daisy: 4   Daffodil: 1
>
> Draw a waffle diagram to show the proportion of people who chose each flower.

Total number of people: 10 + 5 + 4 + 1 = 20 There are 20 people.	Find the total number of people by adding the numbers for each flower. Draw a rectangular grid of squares so that there is one square for each person. 4 × 5 = 20, so you can draw a rectangle that is 5 squares long and 4 squares wide.
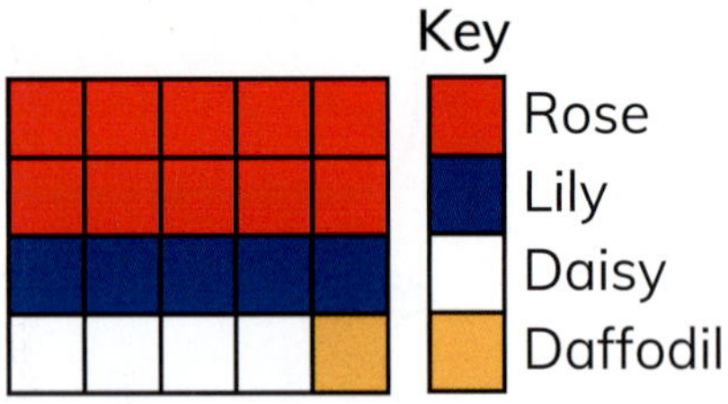 Key: ■ Rose ■ Lily □ Daisy ■ Daffodil	Draw a key showing a colour for each flower. Use the key to colour the squares to show the number of people who chose each flower.

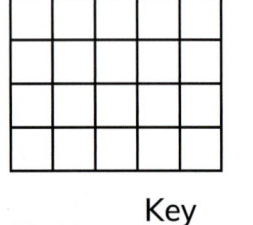

Exercise 12.1

1 This dot plot shows the ages of children visiting a zoo.

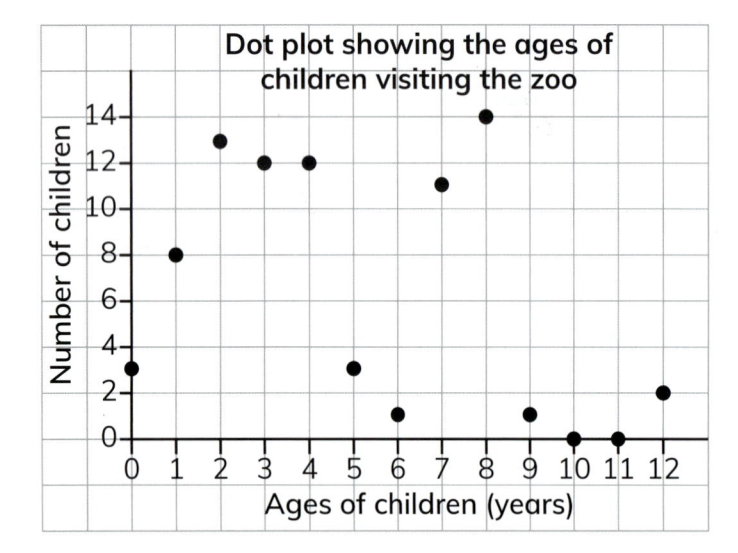

Dot plot showing the ages of children visiting the zoo

(Number of children vs Ages of children (years))

12.1 Representing and interpreting data

a   How many 2 year old children were at the zoo?

b   How many children over 9 years old were at the zoo?

c   The zoo wants to create a new play area for children at the zoo. What ages do you think the play area should be aimed at? Explain your answer using information from the dot plot.

2   Class A and Class B have been collecting and weighing the litter they found around the local area each week for 7 weeks. The classes each recorded the mass of the litter they collected in a bar chart.

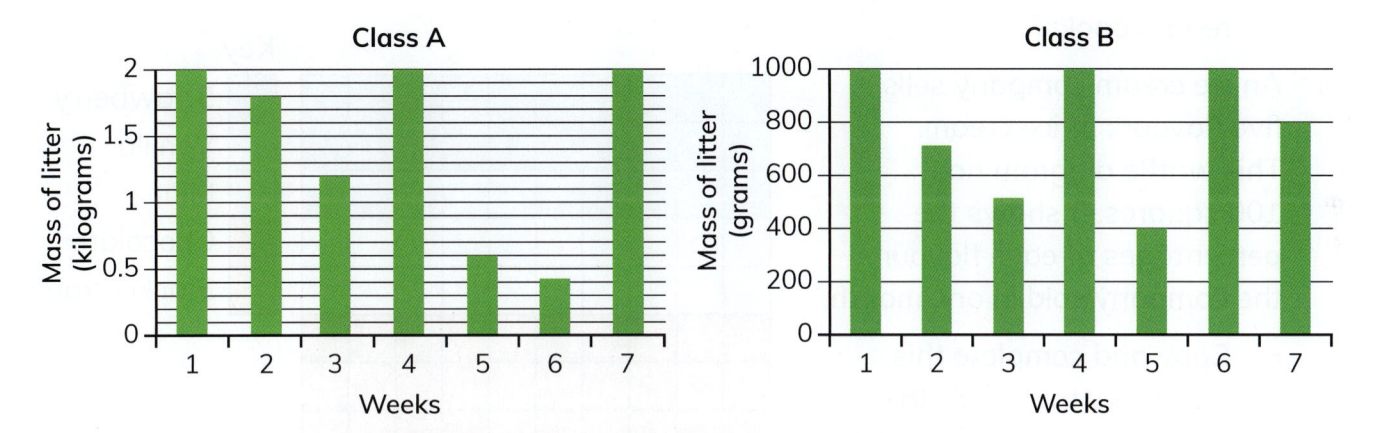

The bar charts use different scales. This makes it difficult to compare the mass of litter collected by each class.

Draw the bar chart for Class B again, but use the same scale as the bar chart for Class A. Your new bar chart will show the mass of litter in kilograms.

Answer these questions, using **your** bar chart for Class B and the bar chart above for Class A:

a   What mass of litter did Class A collect in week 5?

b   What mass of litter did Class B collect in week 5?

c   How much more litter was collected by Class A than Class B in week 7?

d   What mass of litter did both classes collect altogether in week 3?

e   In which week was the least mass of litter collected altogether?

12 Data

3 This waffle diagram shows the number of books 30 people read in one month.

a How many people read 0 books?

b How many people read more than 4 books?

c What fraction of the people read 2 books?

d What percentage of the people read 3 books?

Key
- 0 book
- 1 book
- 2 books
- 3 books
- 4 books
- 5 books

4 An ice cream company sells five flavours of ice cream. This waffle diagram has 100 squares. It shows the percentages of each flavour the company sold in one month.

Key
- Strawberry
- Vanilla
- Mint
- Chocolate
- Blackcurrant

a Copy and complete this frequency table. Use the waffle diagram to complete the percentages of different ice cream flavours sold.

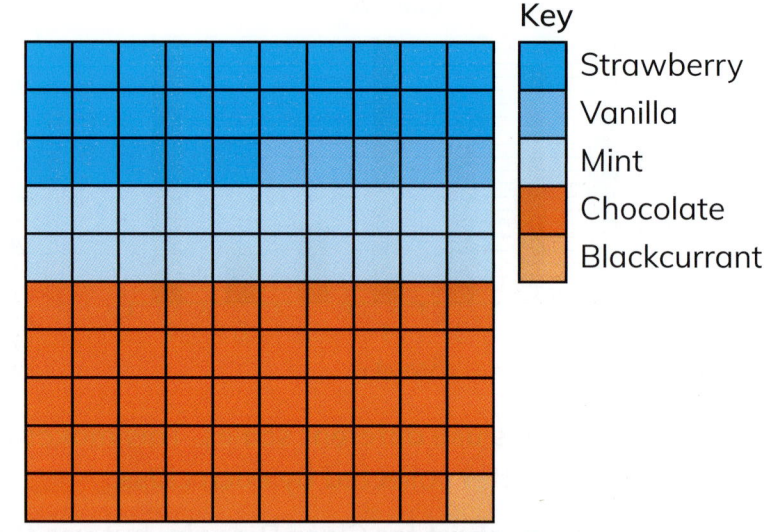

Ice cream flavour	Frequency	Proportion
Strawberry	500	
Vanilla	100	
Mint	400	20%
Chocolate	980	
Blackcurrant	20	

b What percentage of the ice creams sold were **not** chocolate?

12.1 Representing and interpreting data

5   These tally charts show the number of visitors to two hotels.

Hotel Beachfront		
Month	Tally	Number of visitors
Jan	IIII	4
Feb	IIII	4
Mar	HHT I	6
Apr	HHT HHT III	13
May	HHT HHT HHT HHT	20
June	HHT HHT HHT HHT IIII	24
July	HHT HHT HHT HHT HHT HHT	30
Aug	HHT HHT HHT HHT HHT HHT I	31
Sept	HHT HHT HHT HHT II	22
Oct	HHT HHT I	11
Nov	HHT III	8
Dec	IIII	4

Hotel Snowy Mountain		
Month	Tally	Number of visitors
Jan	HHT HHT HHT HHT HHT HHT	
Feb	HHT HHT HHT HHT HHT III	
Mar	HHT HHT HHT HHT II	
Apr	HHT HHT III	
May	HHT HHT	
June	HHT III	
July	HHT III	
Aug	HHT III	
Sept	HHT IIII	
Oct	HHT HHT	
Nov	HHT HHT HHT III	
Dec	HHT HHT HHT HHT HHT III	

a   Copy the tally chart for Hotel Snowy Mountain. Complete the number of visitors for each month at Snowy Mountain.

b   Draw a bar chart of the data for Hotel Beachfront.

c   Describe the pattern in the graph.

d   Draw a dot plot of the data for Hotel Snowy Mountain.

e   Describe the pattern in the graph.

f   Give one explanation for the differences between the data.

12 Data

6 A tour operator has surveyed some people to find out what type of activities they like to do on holiday. This Venn diagram shows the results.

Venn diagram showing which activities some people like to do on holiday

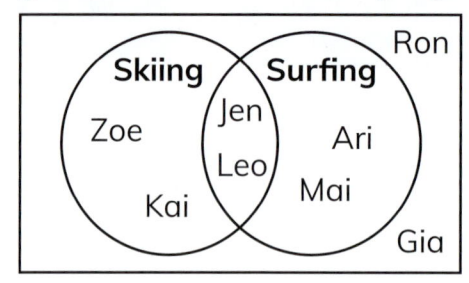

Skiing: Zoe, Kai
Both: Jen, Leo
Surfing: Ari, Mai
Neither: Ron, Gia

The tour operator wants to display the results of their survey in a Carroll diagram.

Draw a Carroll diagram showing the same results as the Venn diagram above.

Think like a mathematician

Work on this investigation with a partner or in a small group.

Hamza is making bracelets for children. He puts a tile on the bracelet for each letter in the child's name so he needs to know how many letters there are in the names.

How many tiles should Hamza put on the bracelets?

Discuss how you will collect data to answer the question. You will need to decide which children, and how many children, you will collect data from.

Collect your data in a table like this.

	Tally	Frequency

Make a dot plot, bar chart or waffle diagram of your data.

You are **convincing** when you use your collected data as evidence for your solution.

Look what I can do!

☐ I can investigate a question by collecting data.

☐ I can represent data using tables, bar charts, dot plots and waffle diagrams.

☐ I can find patterns in data to answer statistical questions.

> 12.2 Frequency diagrams and line graphs

We are going to ...

- investigate questions by collecting data
- represent data using frequency diagrams and line graphs
- find patterns in data to answer statistical questions.

Sometimes the data we collect is as measurements rather than things that are counted or put into categories. The measurements can be compared to solve problems and answer statistical questions.

Think of three questions you might investigate where you would need to collect measurements.

frequency diagram
line graph

Worked example 2

Describe the pattern in the line graph.

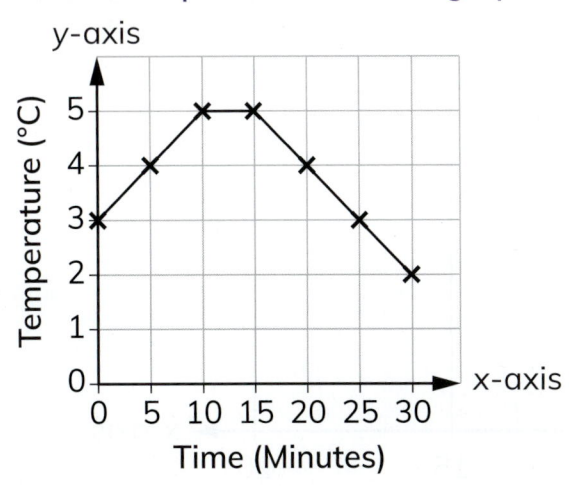

12 Data

Continued

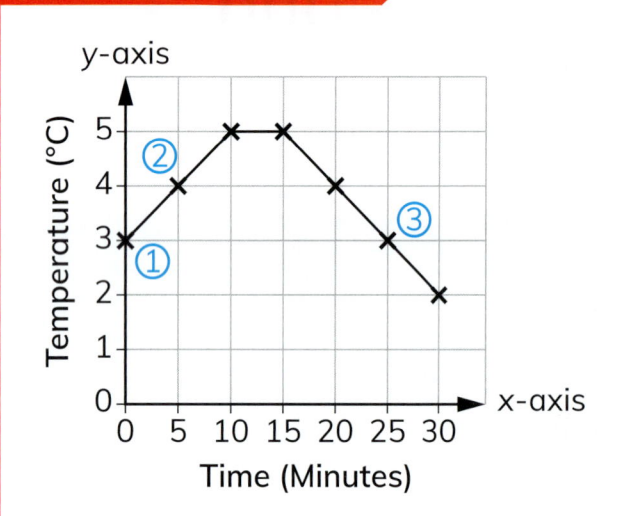

Look at the different sections of the line graph.

Describe the shape of the line on the graph in words. Use words like 'up' and 'down'.

Answer:

The line starts at 3°.

Then the line goes **up** to 5°.

Then the line goes **down** to 2°.

Exercise 12.2

1 This is a frequency diagram showing the times it took runners to complete a race.

12.2 Frequency diagrams and line graphs

a   How many runners took between 15 and 20 minutes to complete the race?

b   How many runners took less than 15 minutes to complete the race?

c   Arun says that the graph shows that the longest time taken to complete the race was 20 minutes. He might not be correct. Explain why he might not be correct.

2   The heights of 20 dogs are measured in centimetres. The results are recorded in a table.

Height in centimetres	Frequency (number of dogs)
30 to less than 40	6
40 to less than 50	7
50 to less than 60	4
60 to less than 70	2
70 to less than 80	1

Copy and complete this frequency diagram using the data in the table.

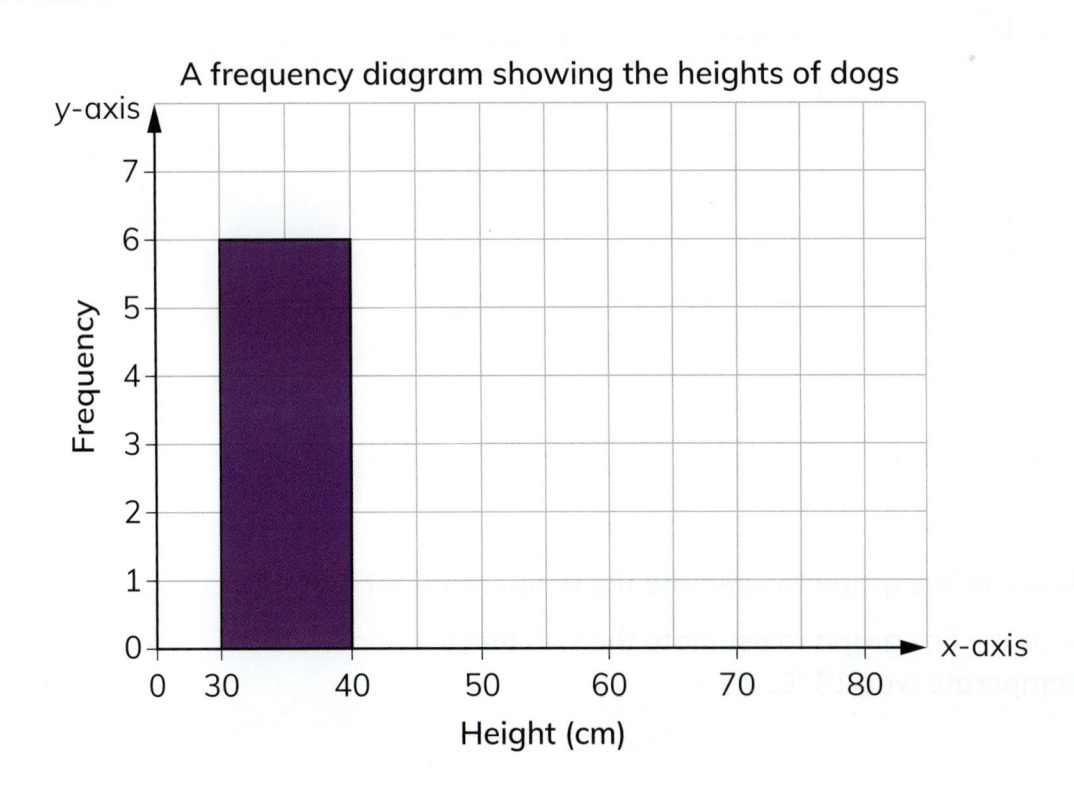

A frequency diagram showing the heights of dogs

139

12 Data

3   a   Describe one way that bar charts and frequency diagrams are different.

   b   Describe one way that bar charts and frequency diagrams are similar.

   c   Discuss the differences and similarities between bar charts and frequency diagrams with a partner. Write down any further differences and similarities you discuss.

4   The temperature in Zoe's playground was measured five times during one day. These are the results.

This line graph shows the results.

Time	Temperature (C°)
9 a.m.	8
11 a.m.	12
1 p.m.	14
3 p.m.	15
5 p.m.	11

A line graph showing the temperature in Zoe's playground

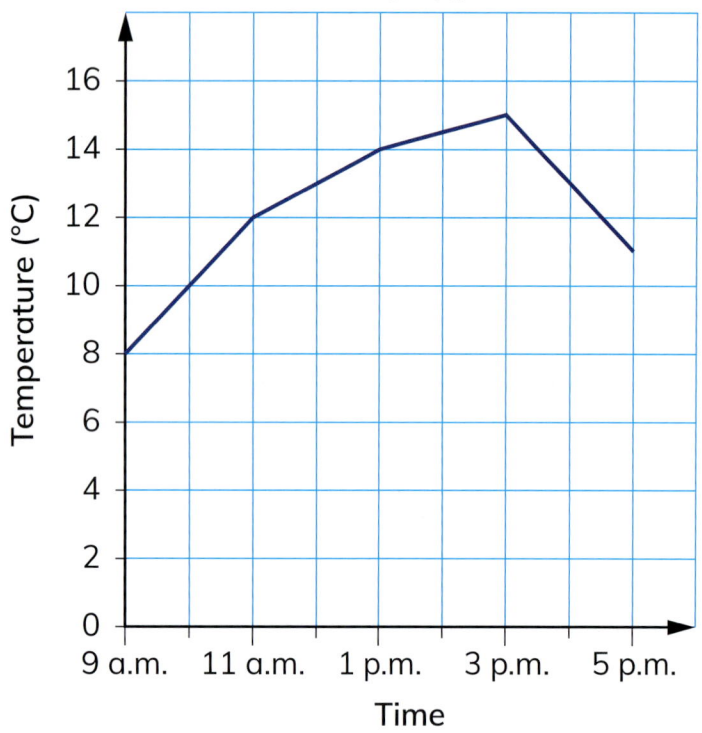

   a   What was the temperature at 5 p.m.?

   b   At what time was the temperature 8 °C?

   c   Use the line graph to estimate the temperature at 10 a.m.

   d   Use the line graph to estimate the two times when the temperate was 13 °C.

12.2 Frequency diagrams and line graphs

5 Mike put two cups of water in different places. He measured the temperature of the water every 10 minutes. These are his results.

Time	Cup 1	Cup 2
0 minutes	10 °C	10 °C
10 minutes	10 °C	9 °C
20 minutes	11 °C	7 °C
30 minutes	12 °C	5 °C
40 minutes	14 °C	4 °C
50 minutes	17 °C	3 °C
60 minutes	18 °C	3 °C

a Draw a line graph showing the temperature of cup 1.

b Draw a line graph showing the temperature of cup 2.

c Describe the pattern on the graph for cup 1.

d Describe the pattern on the graph for cup 2.

e Explain why there might be a different pattern for cup 1 and cup 2.

f Share your explanation with your class. What different explanations do other learners have for the different patterns?

6 Work on this investigation with a partner or in a small group.

Discuss how you will collect data to answer these questions:

How does the temperature change outside your classroom during the day?

How does the temperature change inside your classroom during the day?

Draw a table to collect the data.

Draw two line graphs to display your data.

Describe the pattern in your graph showing the temperature outside your classroom.

Describe the pattern in your graph showing the temperature inside your classroom.

Write about what is similar and different about how the temperature changes outside and inside your classroom during the day.

12 Data

> **Think like a mathematician**
>
> Work with a partner or in a small group. Choose one of these investigations and collect data to answer the question. You could choose a question of your own to investigate. Check your question with your teacher.
>
> - Do nine year olds have longer feet than ten year olds?
> - If you put a stick in the ground outside, how would the length of its shadow change over one day?
> - How does the temperature of an object change on white and black paper left in sunshine?
>
> Discuss what data you will need to collect and how you will collect the data.
>
> Collect your data.
>
> Represent the data you have collected using a frequency diagram or line graph.
>
> Write a sentence answering the question.
>
> Describe any pattern in your data.
>
> Write an explanation for any pattern you find.
>
> - You are **conjecturing** when you think about and write possible explanations for the patterns in your data.
> - You are **critiquing** when you consider whether your choice of graph or chart was the best.

Reflect on your choice of graph or chart in the investigation. Was it the best choice for your data? Why?

Look what I can do!

☐ I can investigate questions by collecting data.

☐ I can represent data using frequency diagrams and line graphs.

☐ I can find patterns in data to answer statistical questions.

12.2 Frequency diagrams and line graphs

Check your progress

1 These are the insects found in 1 hour in a garden.

Type of insect	Beetle	Butterfly	Ladybird	Moth	Wasp
Frequency	20	5	3	2	10

   a Draw a waffle diagram to represent the number of different insects found in the garden.

   b What percentage of the insects found were beetles?

2 The length of children's thumbs were measured in Class A and Class B. These dot plots show the results.

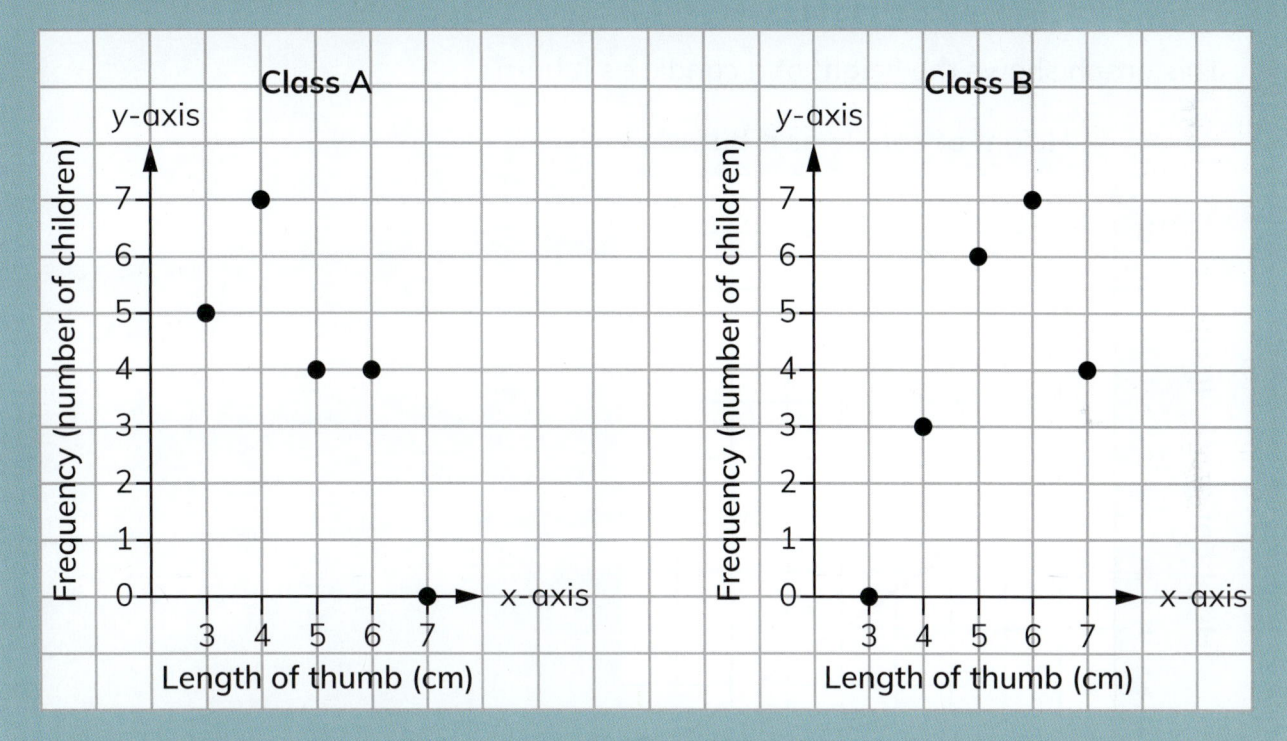

   a Describe the pattern in the dot plot for Class A.

   b Describe the pattern in the dot plot for Class B.

   c Describe the difference in lengths of thumbs for the children in Class A and Class B.

   d What might explain the difference between the length in thumbs for Class A and Class B?

12 Data

Continued

3 This is a table of the mass of parcels loaded into a van.

Mass of the parcels (kg)	Frequency
0 to less than 2	7
2 to less than 4	5
4 to less than 6	4
6 to less than 8	0
8 to less than 10	2

Draw a frequency diagram showing the mass of the parcels.

4 This graph shows the height of a candle as it burns.

Height of candle as it burns

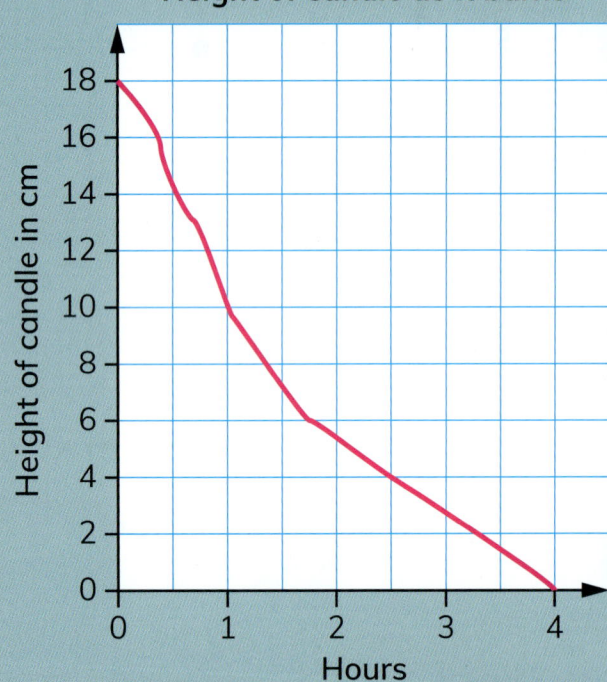

a How tall was the candle when it was first lit?

b How many centimetres of candle burned in the first hour?

c Use the line graph to estimate the height of the candle after 2 hours.

d How long does the candle take to burn down from 18 cm to 4 cm?

Project 4

Depicting data

Some children in Class 5 were asked about their favourite type of fruit. Here are the results:

Type of fruit	Number of children
Pears	11
Oranges	9

Sofia drew a waffle diagram to show these results.

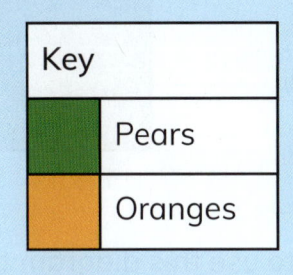

Key:
- Green = Pears
- Orange = Oranges

How easy is it to use this diagram to compare how popular the different fruits are?

Have a go at drawing a clearer waffle diagram to display this data. What did you change? Why?

Marcus drew a bar chart to show these results.

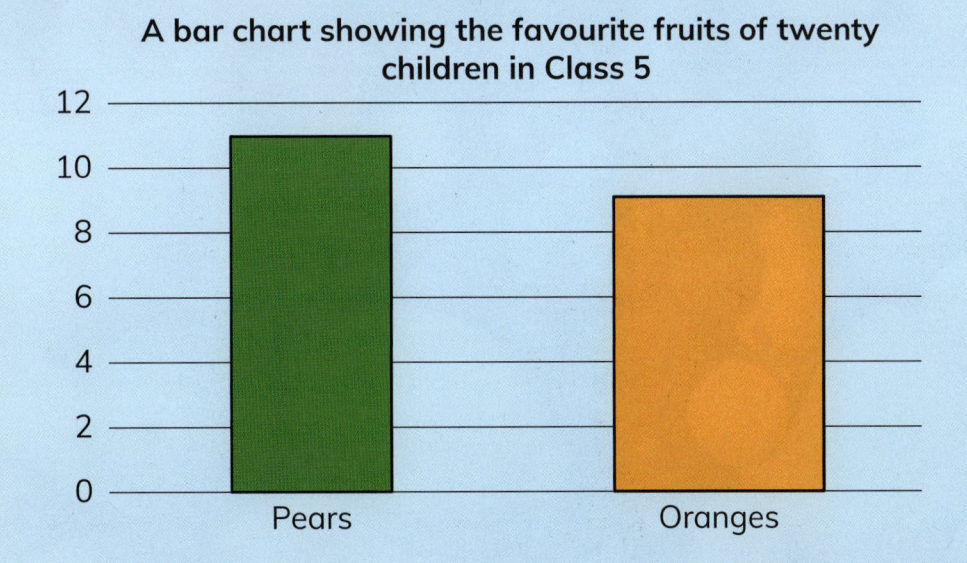

A bar chart showing the favourite fruits of twenty children in Class 5

(Bar chart: Pears = 11, Oranges = 9)

Project 4 Depicting data

> **Continued**
>
> How easy is it to use this diagram to compare how popular the different fruits are?
>
> Have a go at drawing a clearer bar chart to display this data. What did you change? Why?
>
> Zara also drew a bar chart to represent this data.
>
> **A bar chart showing the favourite fruits of twenty children in Class 5**
>
> | | Pears | Oranges |
> |---|---|---|
> | 11 | ■ | |
> | 10 | ■ | |
> | 9 | ■ | ■ |
> | 8 | | |
>
> How easy is it to use this diagram to compare how popular the different fruits are? What could be changed to make this bar chart clearer?

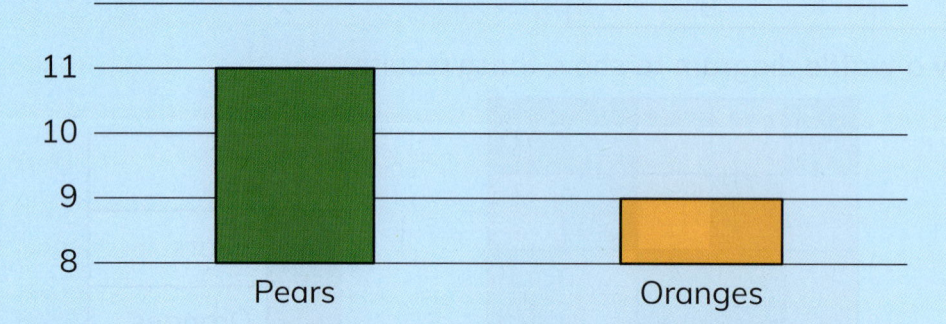

13 > Ratio and proportion

> **Getting started**
>
> 1 Here is a table square.
>
> | × | 1 | 2 | 3 | 4 | 5 |
> |---|---|---|---|---|---|
> | 1 | 1 | 2 | 3 | 4 | 5 |
> | 2 | 2 | 4 | 6 | 8 | 10 |
> | 3 | 3 | 6 | 9 | 12 | 15 |
> | 4 | 4 | 8 | 12 | 16 | 20 |
> | 5 | 5 | 10 | 15 | 20 | 25 |
>
> The first two rows show a set of equivalent fractions.
>
> $\frac{1}{2} = \frac{2}{4} = \frac{3}{6} = \frac{4}{8} = \frac{5}{10}$
>
> Find the following equivalent fractions.
>
> a $\frac{3}{4} = \frac{6}{\Box}$
>
> b $\frac{2}{5} = \frac{\Box}{10}$
>
> 2 Copy and complete the list of equivalent fractions.
>
> $\frac{2}{3} = \frac{4}{\Box} = \frac{\Box}{9} = \frac{8}{\Box} = \frac{12}{\Box}$
>
> 3 Find the missing number.
>
> $\frac{6}{\Box} = 50\%$

13 Ratio and proportion

> **Continued**
>
> 4 Copy and complete the table to show equivalent fractions and percentages.
>
> | Fraction | Percentage |
> |---|---|
> | $\frac{1}{2}$ | |
> | | 10% |
> | $\frac{9}{10}$ | |

When things are in proportion they are similar to each other. The only difference is the size.

An architect and a jeweller use proportion in their work.

An architect makes a model of a building before the builders construct the building.

The model and the actual building look the same but they are a different size.

The model is a fraction of the size of the real building.

A jeweller makes necklaces. He works out the proportion of beads in each colour in each pattern.

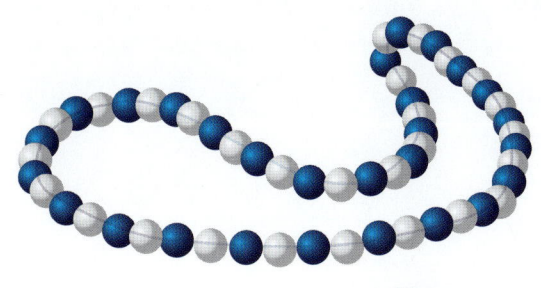

$\frac{1}{2}$ the beads are blue.

$\frac{1}{2}$ the beads are white.

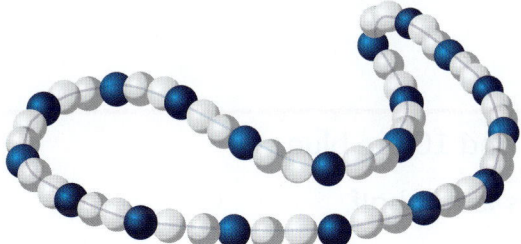

$\frac{1}{3}$ of the beads are blue.

$\frac{2}{3}$ of the beads are white.

> 13.1 Ratio and proportion

We are going to ...

- use the language 'in every' and 'out of' to discuss proportion
- use the language 'for every' to discuss ratio
- use the notation : to show ratios.

proportion
ratio

Ratio is used to compare two or more quantities.

Look at this necklace.

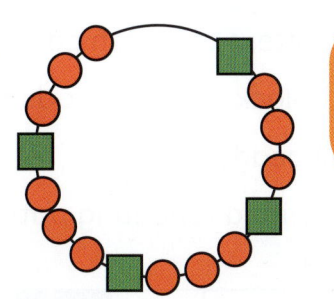

The ratio of circles to squares is 3 : 1

The ratio of squares to circles is 1 : 3

The ratio must be written in the correct order.

Can you find examples of two quantities that can be compared using a ratio?

13 Ratio and proportion

Worked example 1

There are 10 blue boats and 20 red boats on the lake.

Is each statement true or false?

a   10 out of 30 boats are blue.

b   Half of the boats are red.

c $\frac{2}{3}$ of the boats are red.

d $\frac{1}{10}$ of the boats are blue.

e   The ratio of red boats to blue boats is 10 : 20.

a	True	There are 30 boats altogether and 10 are blue.
b	False	20 out of 30 boats are red. This is not half.
c	True	20 out of 30 boats are red.
		$\frac{20}{30} = \frac{2}{3}$ of the boats are red.
		(This compares part to whole, so is proportion.)
d	False	There are 10 blue boats, but this is $\frac{1}{3}$ of the total.
		(This compares part to whole, so is proportion.)
e	False	The ratio of red boats to blue boats is 20 : 10. The order of a ratio is important.
		(This compares part to part, so is ratio.)

Exercise 13.1

1   Draw a bead pattern to match each of these descriptions.

   a   For every 1 black bead, 3 beads are white.

   b   1 in every 4 beads is white.

2   Imagine a row with a repeating pattern of 3 white squares and 1 black square.

   Is each statement true or false?

   Correct any statements that are false.

13.1 Ratio and proportion

   a 3 out of 4 squares are black.
   b $\frac{3}{4}$ of the squares are white.
   c The ratio of white squares to black squares is 3 : 4.
   d The ratio of black squares to white squares is 1 : 3.
   e 1 in every 4 squares is black.

3 Zara has 10 blue pens and 5 red pens.

   Write whether each statement is true or false.

   a $\frac{1}{3}$ of the pens are red.
   b The ratio of red pens to blue pens is 10 : 5.
   c 50% of the pens are red.
   d 1 in every 3 pens is red.

   Check your answers to questions 1 to 3 with your partner.
   Discuss any answers that you do not agree on.

4 A bag contains 2 orange counters, 3 blue counters and 5 green counters.

   a What is the ratio of orange : blue : green?
   b What is the ratio of blue : green : orange?
   c What is the ratio of green : blue : orange?
   d What proportion of the counters are blue?
      Write your answer as a fraction and as a percentage.

5 Here is a recipe for pasta sauce.

   a What is the ratio of onions : tomatoes : mushrooms?
   b What is the ratio of tomatoes : mushrooms : onions?
   c What proportion of the recipe is tomatoes?
      Write your answer as a fraction.

   Pasta sauce
   1 cup mushrooms
   2 cups onions
   4 cups tomatoes

6 Here is a string of grey and white beads.

   What proportion of the beads are grey?
   Give your answer as a fraction.

7 Sofia says her diagram shows black circles and white circles in the ratio 1 : 3.

   Sofia is not correct.

   Explain how she can correct her answer.

13 Ratio and proportion

Think back over the work you have done on ratio and proportion. What have you learned? Is there anything you need to get better at?

Think like a mathematician

a How tall do you think the cactus is?

If the person is 160 cm tall, how tall is the cactus?

b Four girls describe a fruit smoothie made of kiwis and bananas. Three of the descriptions are right, but one is wrong. Which girl is wrong?

Alana: $\frac{3}{10}$ of the smoothie is banana.

Fatima: For every 2 kiwis there is 1 banana.

Haibo: For every 3 bananas there are 7 kiwis.

Orla: 70% of the smoothie is kiwi.

If you explain your results, you will show you are **convincing**.

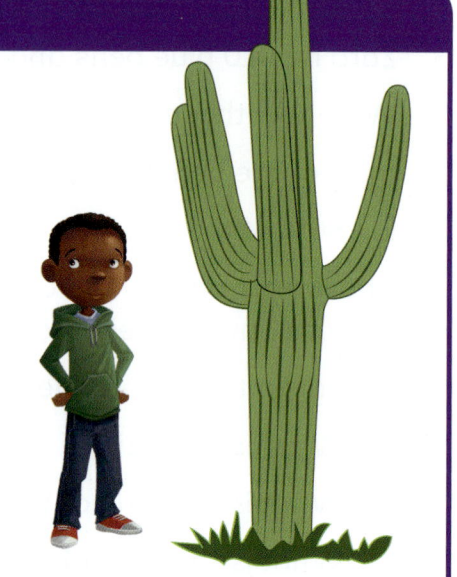

Look what I can do!

☐ I can use the language 'in every' and 'out of' to discuss proportions.
☐ I can use the language 'for every' to discuss ratio.
☐ I can use the notation : to show ratios.

13.1 Ratio and proportion

Check your progress

1 Sue is a decorator. She mixes paint to make new colours.

   She uses 1 can of blue paint and 2 cans of yellow paint to make green paint.

   She uses 3 cans of red paint and 4 cans of blue paint to make purple paint.

   Write whether each statement is true or false. Correct any statements that are false.

   a The ratio of yellow to blue in green paint is 1 : 2
   b The proportion of red in the purple paint is $\frac{4}{7}$
   c $\frac{2}{3}$ of green paint is yellow
   d 3 in every 4 parts of purple paint is red
   e $\frac{1}{3}$ of green paint is blue

2 Marcus says, 'My diagram shows 1 out of every 2 shapes is a triangle.'

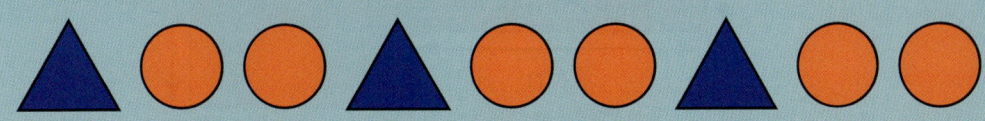

   Explain why Marcus might think he is correct.

   What should Marcus have written?

14　Area and perimeter

Getting started

1. Count squares to estimate the area of this lake.

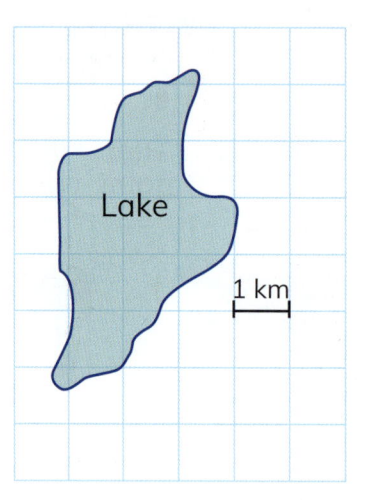

2. a. What is the area of the yellow rectangle?
   b. What is the perimeter of the yellow rectangle?

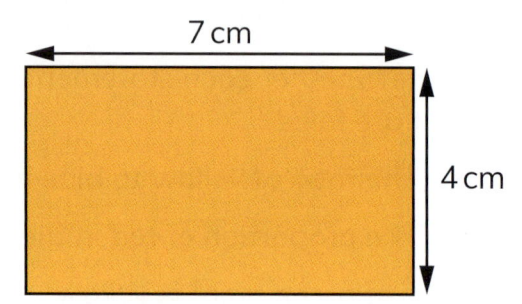

   (7 cm by 4 cm)

3. What is the total area of this shape?

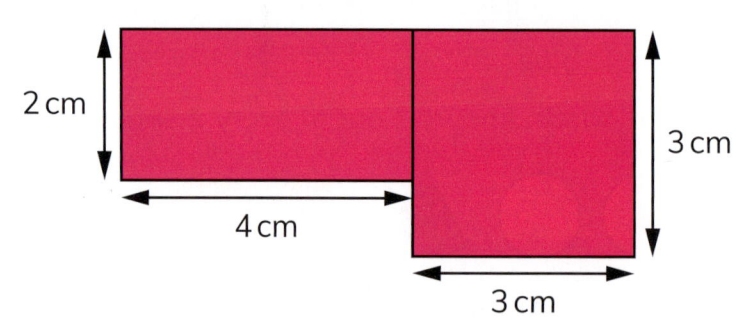

   (2 cm, 4 cm, 3 cm, 3 cm)

14.1 Area and perimeter

Being able to estimate and calculate areas and perimeters is very useful in everyday life.

Prices for carpets are calculated using square metres.

How could you estimate and work out the price to cover your classroom floor with one of these carpets?

$30 per m^2

$32 per m^2

$20 per m^2

$25 per m^2

> ## 14.1 Area and perimeter

We are going to …

- estimate and measure the perimeter of 2D shapes
- estimate and measure the area of 2D shapes
- work out the perimeter and area of shapes made from two rectangles.

The shape of a garden is not always a rectangle. Knowing how to work out the perimeter of different shapes can help you to solve problems in everyday life.

area

perimeter

14 Area and perimeter

How can you work out the number of fence panels you need to go around this garden?

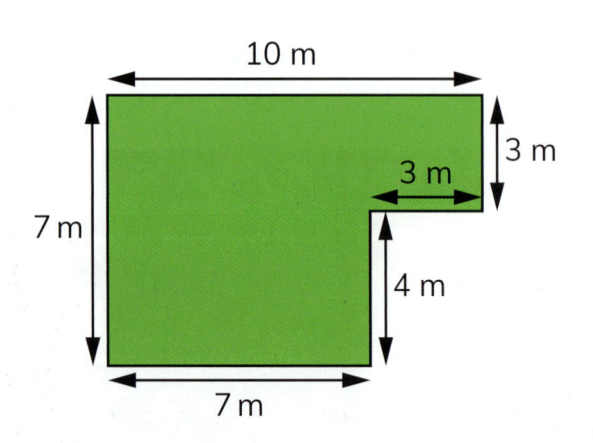

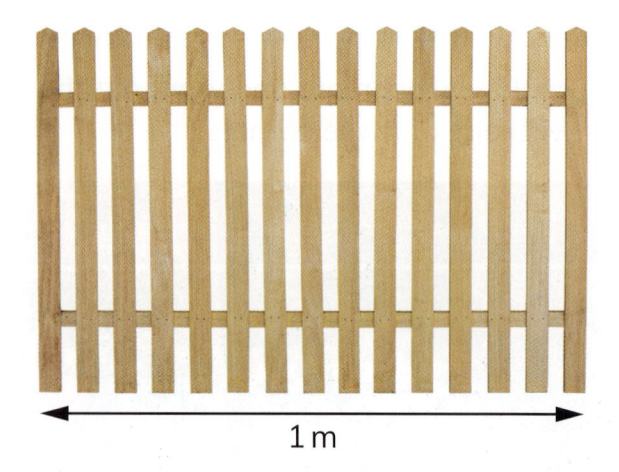

Exercise 14.1

1   a   Measure the perimeter of the blue triangle.

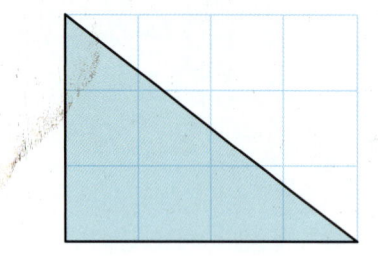

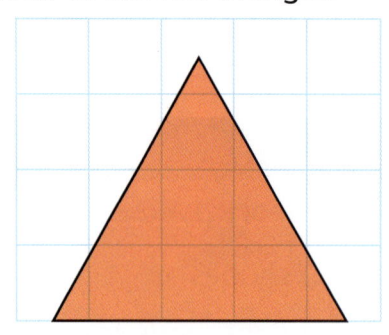

> **Tip**
>
> Area is measured in square units, for example cm² or m². Perimeter is measured in units of length, for example cm or m.

   b   Estimate the area of the blue triangle.

   c   Measure the perimeter of the red triangle.

   d   Estimate the area of the red triangle.

   e   Copy and complete this sentence using the words 'areas' and 'perimeters'.

   The blue and red triangles have the same _____, but different _____.

   f   Draw a rectangle with the same perimeter as the blue triangle.

   g   Draw a rectangle with the same area as the blue triangle.

14.1 Area and perimeter

2   a   Estimate the perimeter of this shape.

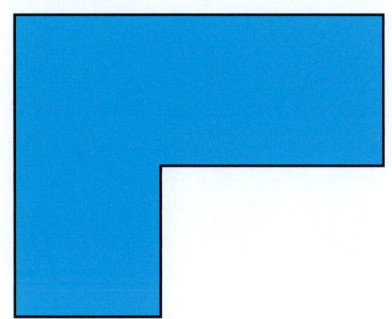

    b   Measure the perimeter of the shape.

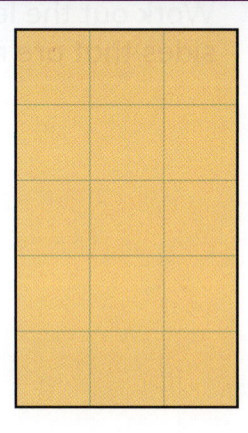

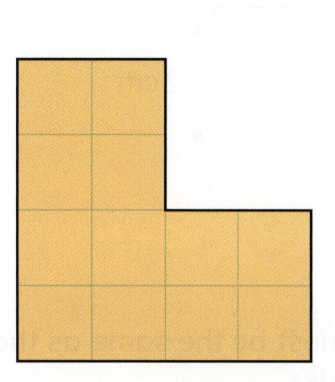

> **Think like a mathematician**
>
> Both of these polygons have a perimeter of 16 cm, but they have different areas.
>
> On 1 cm squared paper, use the lines to draw some other polygons like these that have a perimeter of 16 cm. Label each shape with its area.
>
> Using a whole number of centimetres on each side of a polygon, what is the smallest area you can make with a perimeter of 16 cm? What is the largest area you can make with a perimeter of 16 cm?
>
> You are **specialising** when you draw and test a polygon to check whether it satisfies the criteria.

Think about how to explain that two shapes can have the same perimeter but different areas. Write down your thoughts. You are **convincing** when you explain this idea.

14 Area and perimeter

Worked example 1

What is the perimeter of this shape?

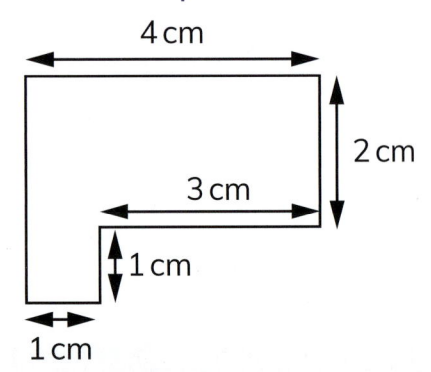

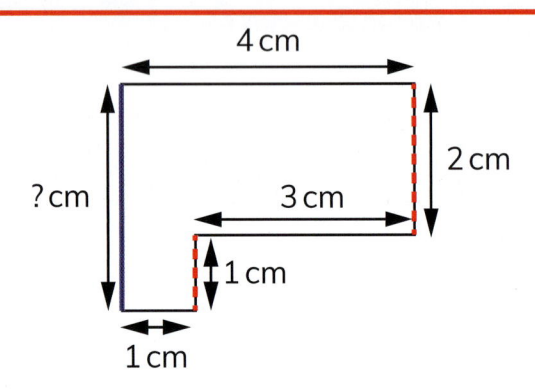

[Shape: L-shaped figure with top side 4 cm, right side 2 cm, inner horizontal 3 cm, inner vertical 1 cm, bottom-left horizontal 1 cm]

Work out the length of any sides that are not labelled.

[Shape repeated with ? cm on the left side]

The unknown side must be the same as the total of the two dotted sides.

2 cm + 1 cm = 3 cm

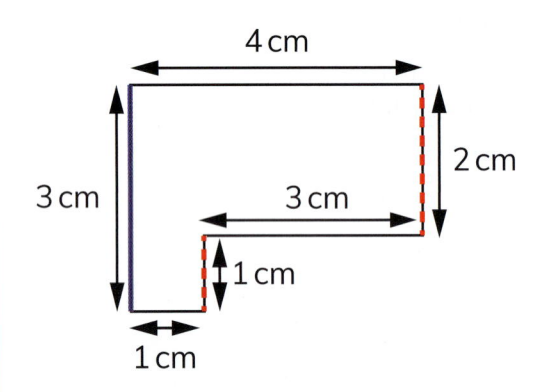

[Shape with left side labelled 3 cm]

Add together the lengths of all the sides.

4 cm + 2 cm + 3 cm + 1 cm + 1 cm + 3 cm = 14 cm

Answer: The perimeter of the shape is 14 cm.

158

14.1 Area and perimeter

3 Find the missing length on each shape.

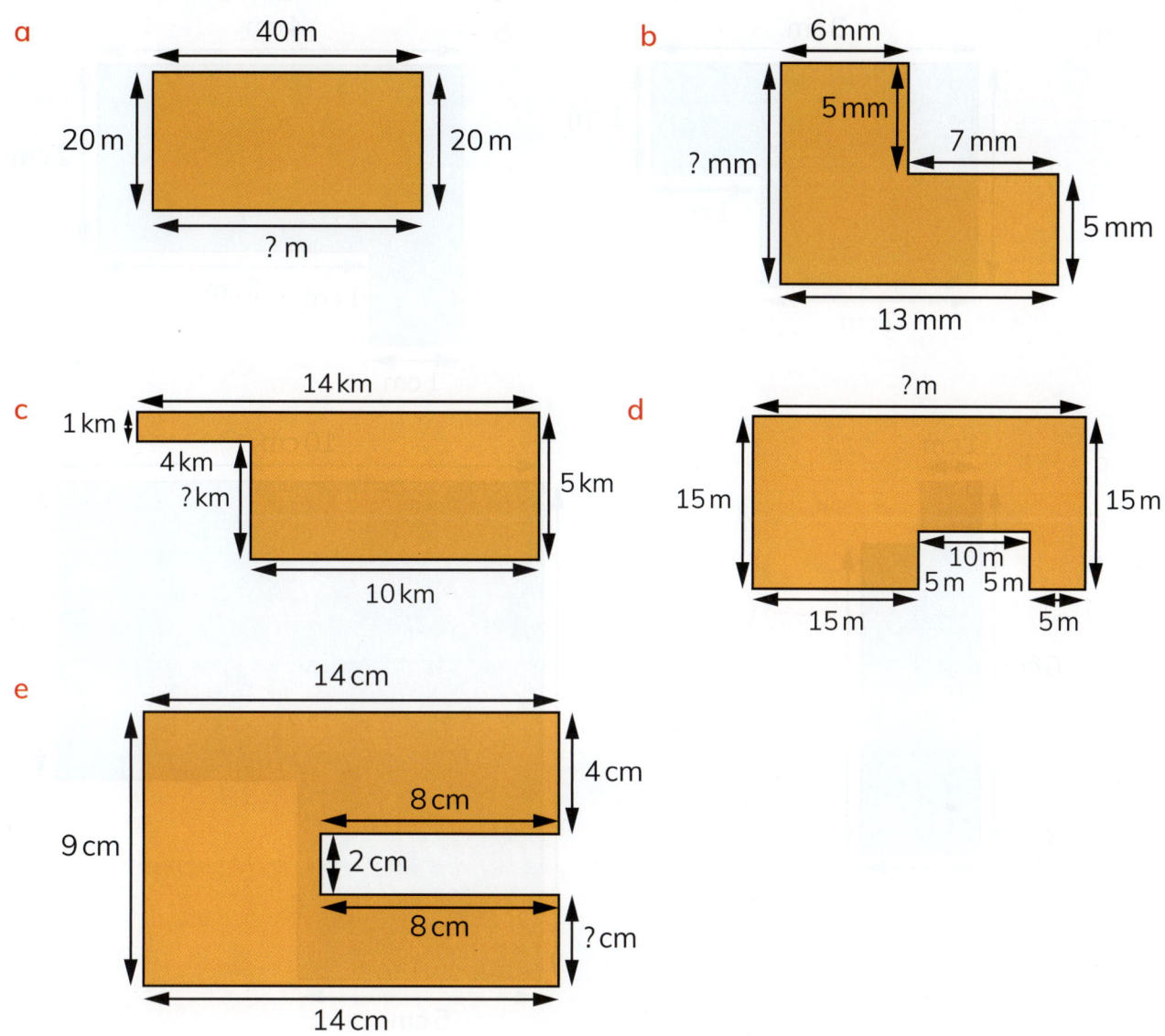

a
40 m
20 m
20 m
? m

b
6 mm
5 mm
7 mm
? mm
5 mm
13 mm

c
14 km
1 km
4 km
? km
5 km
10 km

d
? m
15 m
15 m
10 m
5 m   5 m
15 m
5 m

e
14 cm
4 cm
8 cm
9 cm
2 cm
8 cm
? cm
14 cm

4 Work out the perimeter of each shape in question 3.

14 Area and perimeter

5 Work out the perimeter of these shapes.

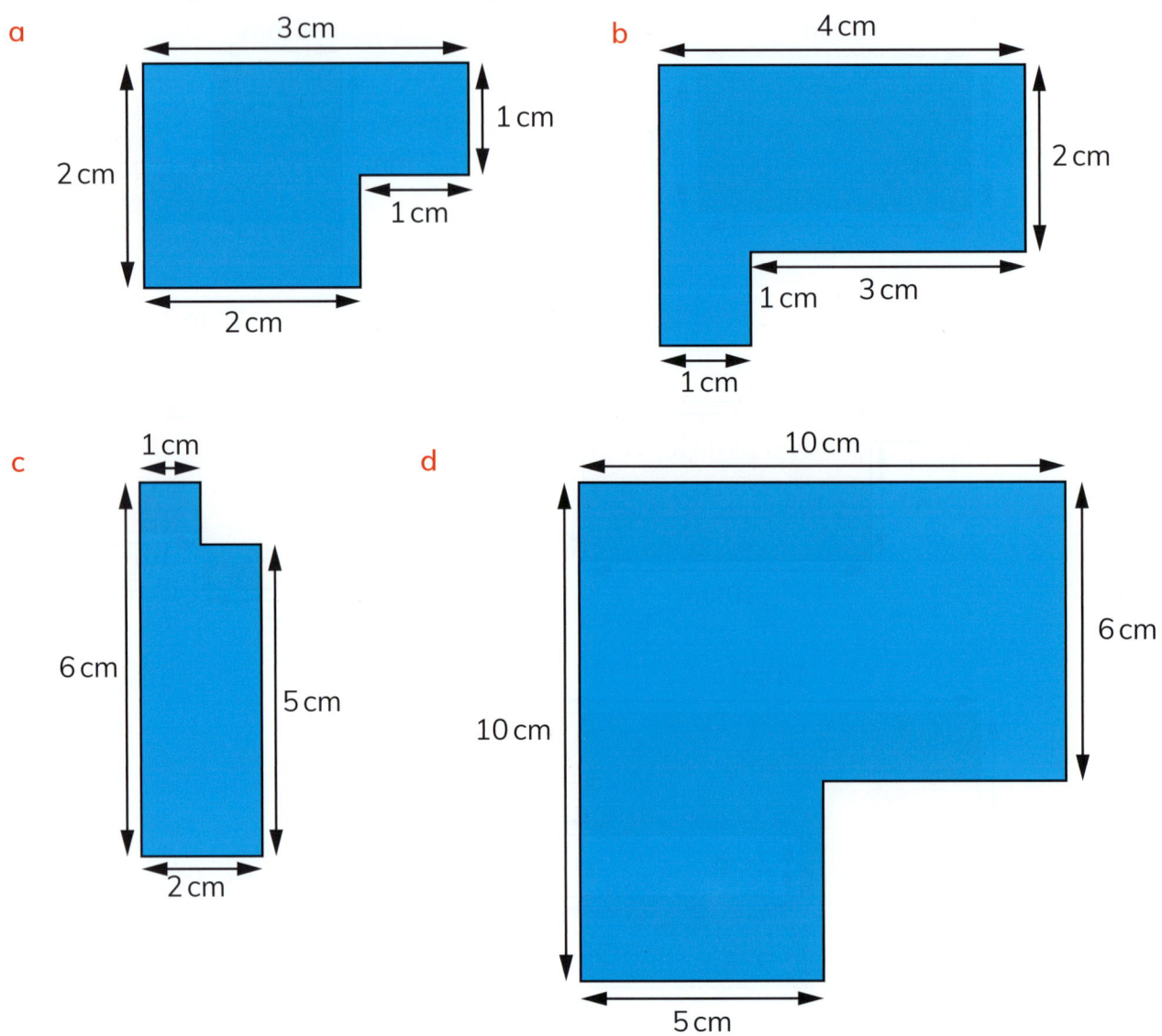

a — 3 cm, 1 cm, 2 cm, 1 cm, 2 cm

b — 4 cm, 2 cm, 3 cm, 1 cm, 1 cm

c — 1 cm, 6 cm, 5 cm, 2 cm

d — 10 cm, 6 cm, 10 cm, 5 cm

6 Which two green rectangles from A–F can you use to make shapes a, b and c?

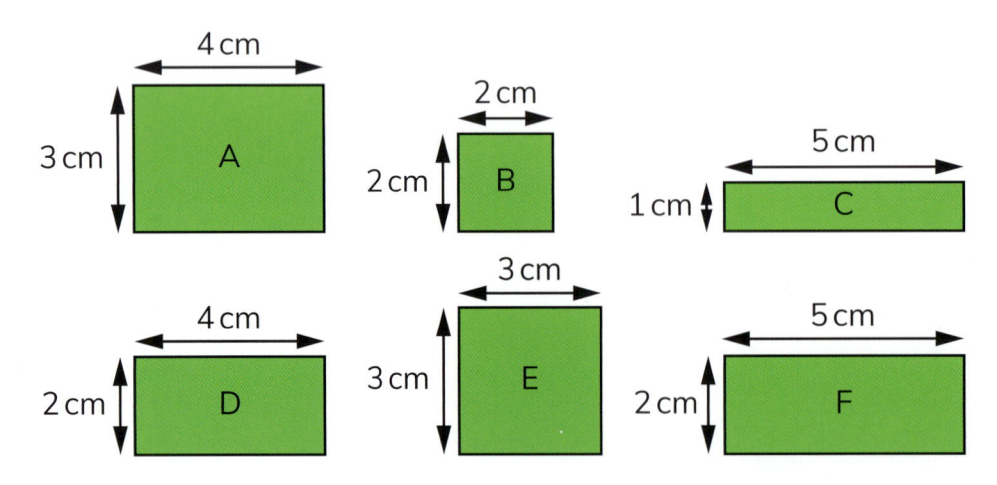

A: 4 cm × 3 cm
B: 2 cm × 2 cm
C: 5 cm × 1 cm
D: 4 cm × 2 cm
E: 3 cm × 3 cm
F: 5 cm × 2 cm

14.1 Area and perimeter

a [shape with dimensions: 2 cm, 3 cm, 2 cm, 3 cm, 1 cm, 5 cm]

b [shape with dimensions: 4 cm, 4 cm, 2 cm, 1 cm, 2 cm, 5 cm]

c [shape with dimensions: 6 cm, 3 cm, 4 cm, 3 cm, 1 cm, 3 cm]

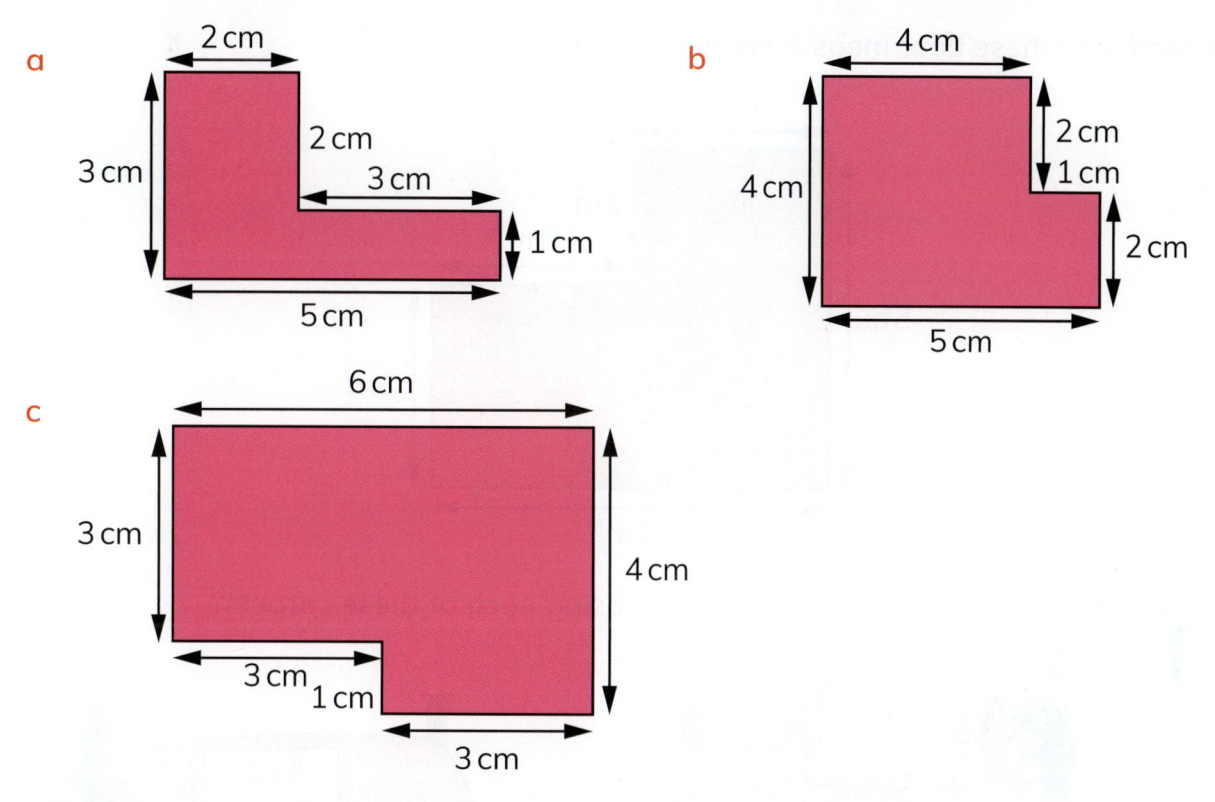

7 Sketch these shapes on plain paper. Divide the shapes into two rectangles. Work out the area of each rectangle.

What is the total area of each shape?

a [shape with dimensions: 5 m, 5 m, 2 m, 4 m, 3 m, 9 m]

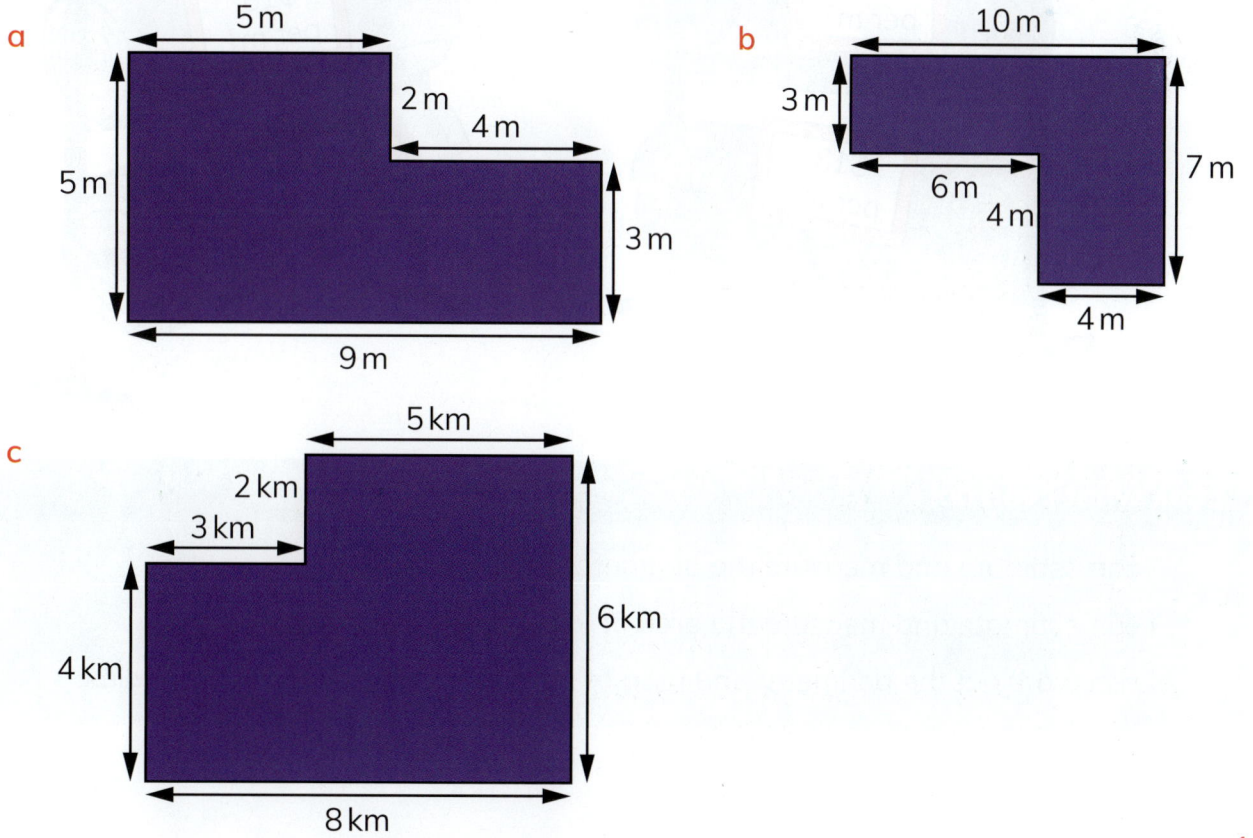

b [shape with dimensions: 10 m, 3 m, 6 m, 7 m, 4 m, 4 m]

c [shape with dimensions: 5 km, 2 km, 3 km, 6 km, 4 km, 8 km]

161

14 Area and perimeter

8 A room has these floor measurements.

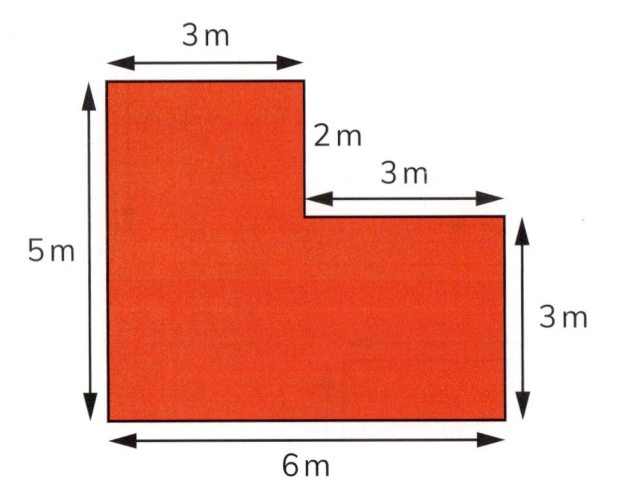

How much does it cost to cover the room using each of these carpets?

$18 per m²

$16 per m²

$13 per m²

$12 per m²

$15 per m²

$21 per m²

Look what I can do!
☐ I can estimate and measure the perimeter of 2D shapes.
☐ I can estimate and measure the area of 2D shapes.
☐ I can work out the perimeter and area of shapes made from two rectangles.

14.1 Area and perimeter

Check your progress

1 a Estimate the perimeter of this shape.

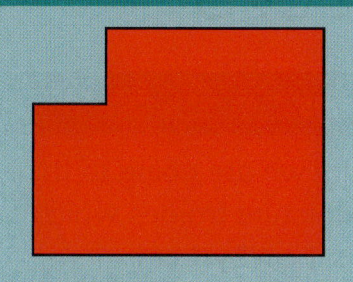

   b Measure the perimeter of the shape.

2 What is the length of the unlabelled side on each shape?

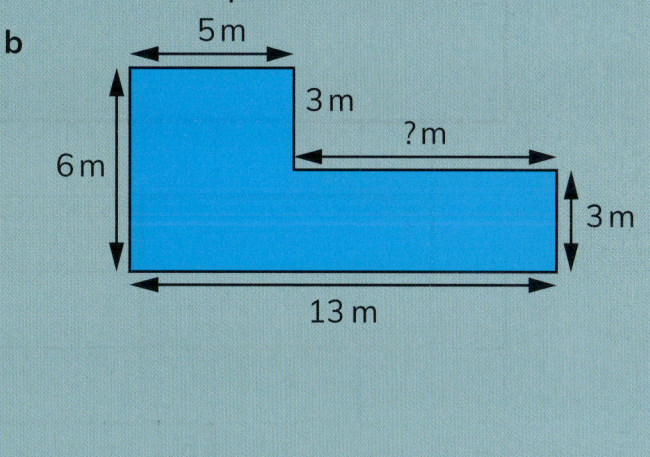

   a (orange shape: ?m top, 5m left, 7m right, 4m and 2m along bottom step, 2m bottom)

   b (blue shape: 5m top, 3m, ?m, 6m left, 3m right, 13m bottom)

3 Work out the area and the perimeter of each shape.

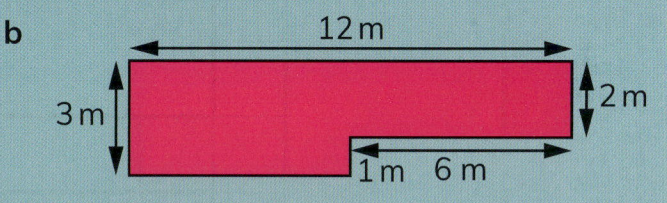

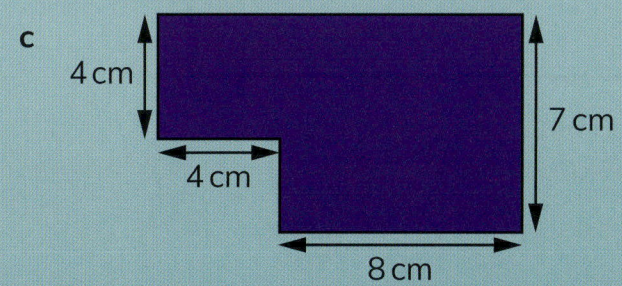

   a (green shape: 1km top, 1km, 2km, 1km left, 2km bottom)

   b (pink shape: 12m top, 3m left, 2m right, 1m, 6m along bottom step)

   c (purple shape: 4cm, 4cm, 7cm, 8cm)

4 Draw two rectangles that have the same area but a different perimeter. Label each rectangle with its area and perimeter.

163

Project 5 Picture frames

Project 5

Picture frames

In this activity we are going to think about rectangular picture frames. Here are six picture frames which are placed on a grid. Each square in this grid is 1 cm by 1 cm.

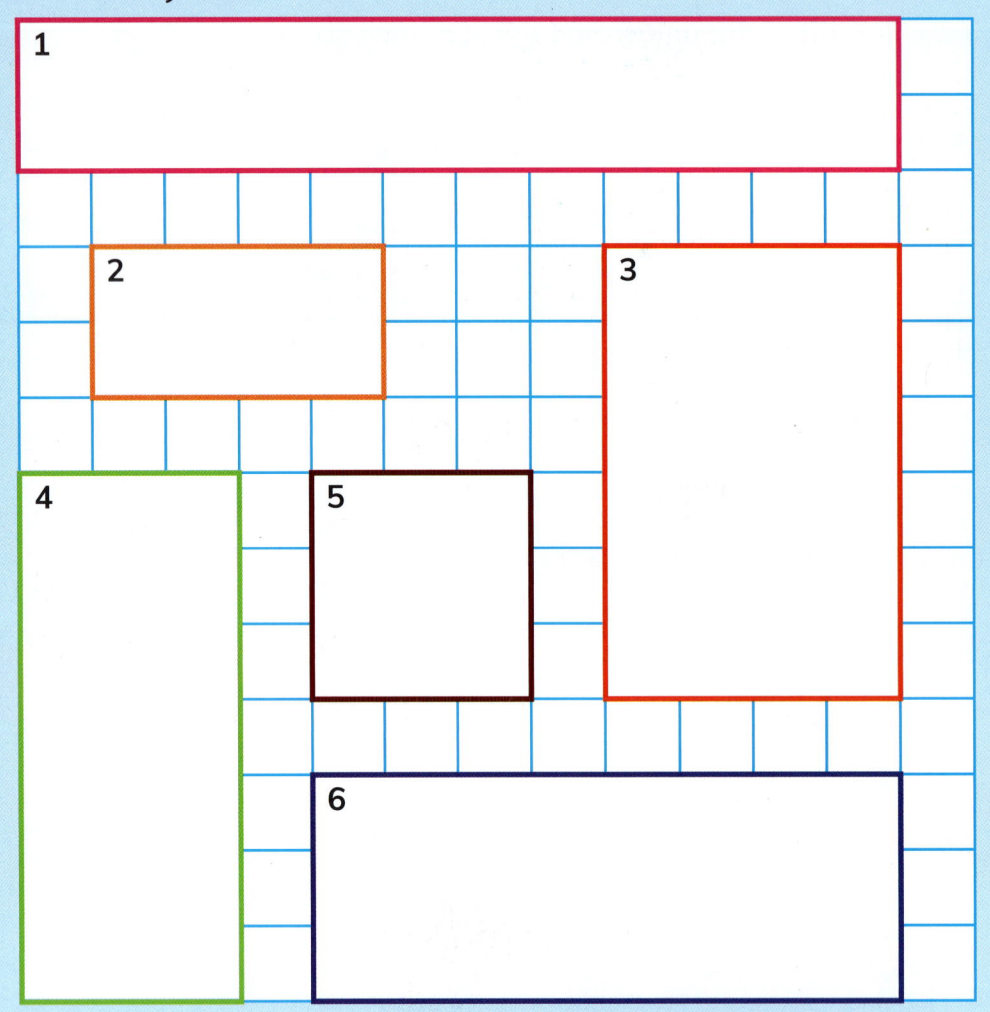

1. Look at all six picture frames. Without counting or measuring, can you guess which frames have the same area?

2. Just by looking, without counting or measuring, can you guess which frames have the same perimeter?

3. Find a way of checking your answer to question 1. Were you correct? Which frames do have the same area?

Project 5: Picture frames

Continued

4 Find a way of checking your answer to question 2. Were you correct? Which frames do have the same perimeter?

5 What is the perimeter of each frame in centimetres?

6 What is the area of each frame in square centimetres?

7 Now imagine that you can take each frame apart at the corners, getting four parts from each frame. You can put all of these parts together to make a new big rectangular frame.

   a What could the area of this new frame be?

   b How can you arrange all of the parts to make a frame with the smallest possible area?

   c How can you make a frame with the largest possible area?

15 Multiplying and dividing fractions and decimals

Getting started

1 The fraction $\frac{1}{2}$ is shaded on the fraction wall.

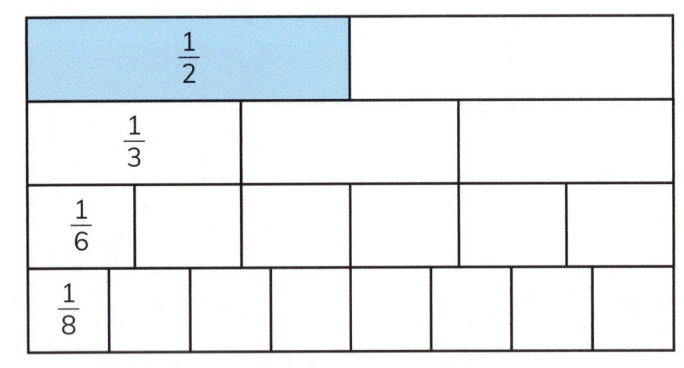

   [fraction wall showing $\frac{1}{2}$, $\frac{1}{3}$, $\frac{1}{6}$, $\frac{1}{8}$]

   Write two different fractions equivalent to $\frac{1}{2}$.

2 These fractions have the same denominator. Write the missing fraction.

   $\frac{4}{9} + \frac{2}{9} + \boxed{} = \frac{8}{9}$

3 Leroy calculates 18×5 using factors.

   He spills ink on his work. What number is under the ink blots?

   $18 = 9 \times \blacksquare$
   so $18 \times 5 = 9 \times \blacksquare \times 5$
   $= 9 \times 10$
   $= 90$

4 Calculate.
   a 3.4×10
   b 68×7

5 Find the missing numbers.
   a $58 \div \boxed{} = 5.8$
   b $12.7 = \boxed{} \div 10$

15 Multiplying and dividing fractions and decimals

These pictures are all about fractions and decimals and how we use them in our everyday life.

Discuss with your partner when you see or use fractions or decimals. Try to think of times when you multiply or divide, for example, when you know the cost of one item and you need to buy three items.

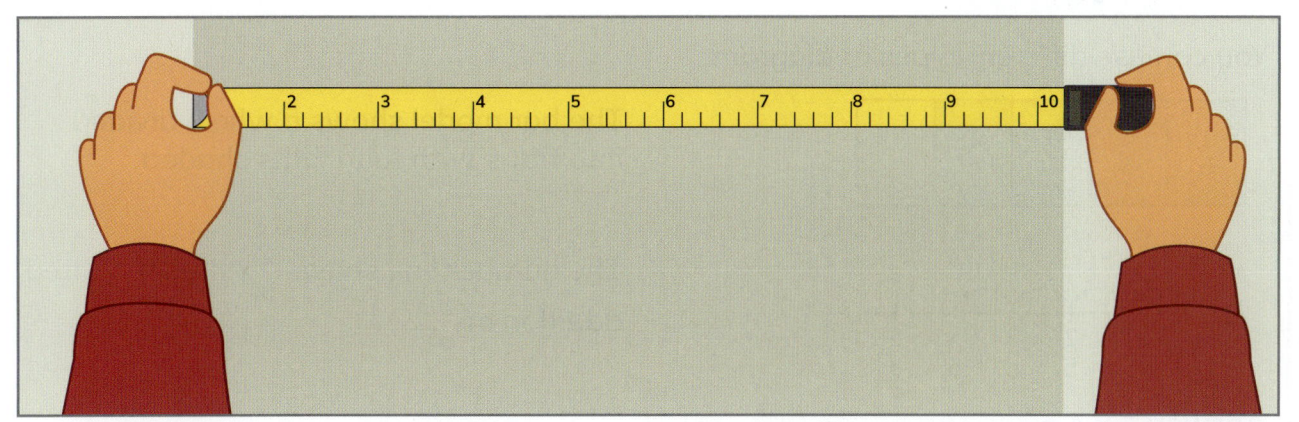

Recipe
Sponge cake

$\frac{3}{4}$ cup butter

1 cup sugar

3 eggs

$1\frac{1}{2}$ cup flour

KG SHOP
1. Shirt $4.60
2. Trousers $9.40
3. T-Shirt $2.75
4. Shoes $5.35

DISCOUNT $2.10
TOTAL $20.00

THANK YOU

AK SHOPPEE
RT ROAD

COMPARE AT $20.00

$12.99

1/2 PRICE SALE

167

15 Multiplying and dividing fractions and decimals

> 15.1 Multiplying and dividing fractions

> **We are going to …**
> - multiply a unit fraction by a whole number
> - divide a unit fraction by a whole number.

Look at the pictures. They show:

$\frac{1}{2} \times 2 = \frac{2}{2} = 1$

$\frac{1}{3} \times 3 = \frac{3}{3} = 1$

$\frac{1}{4} \times 4 = \frac{4}{4} = 1$

Imagine you have $\frac{1}{2}$ an apple and you share it with four friends.

Can you write a calculation to show how much orange you each have?

In this section you will learn how to multiply and divide unit fractions.

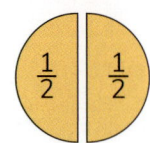

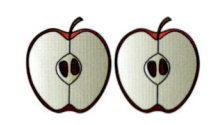

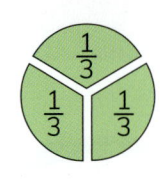

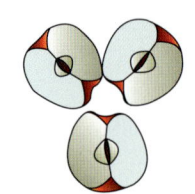

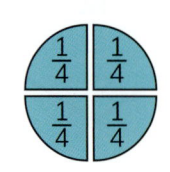

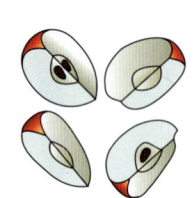

repeated addition
unit fraction

Worked example 1

Calculate $\frac{1}{5} \times 4$

Draw a diagram to show your answer.

You can use different types of diagram.

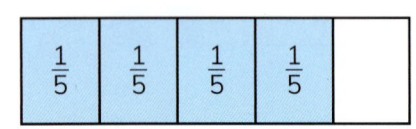

| $\frac{1}{5}$ | $\frac{1}{5}$ | $\frac{1}{5}$ | $\frac{1}{5}$ | |

The bar model shows a whole divided into fifths with four-fifths shaded.

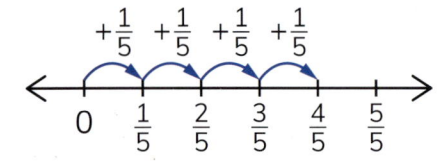

The number line shows $\frac{1}{5} \times 4$ as repeated addition of $\frac{1}{5}$.

Answer: $\frac{1}{5} \times 4 = \frac{4}{5}$

15.1 Multiplying and dividing fractions

Exercise 15.1

1 Calculate $\frac{1}{4} \times 3$. Draw a diagram to show your answer.

2 Calculate $\frac{1}{5} \times 6$. Draw a diagram to show your answer.

3 Amy, Kiki and Magda work out $\frac{1}{6} \times 4$. Here are their methods.

> **Tip**
>
> Estimate your answer before you calculate it. This will help you to spot if you make a mistake in your calculation.

Amy

$\frac{1}{6} \times 4 = \frac{1}{6} + \frac{1}{6} + \frac{1}{6} + \frac{1}{6} = \frac{4}{6}$

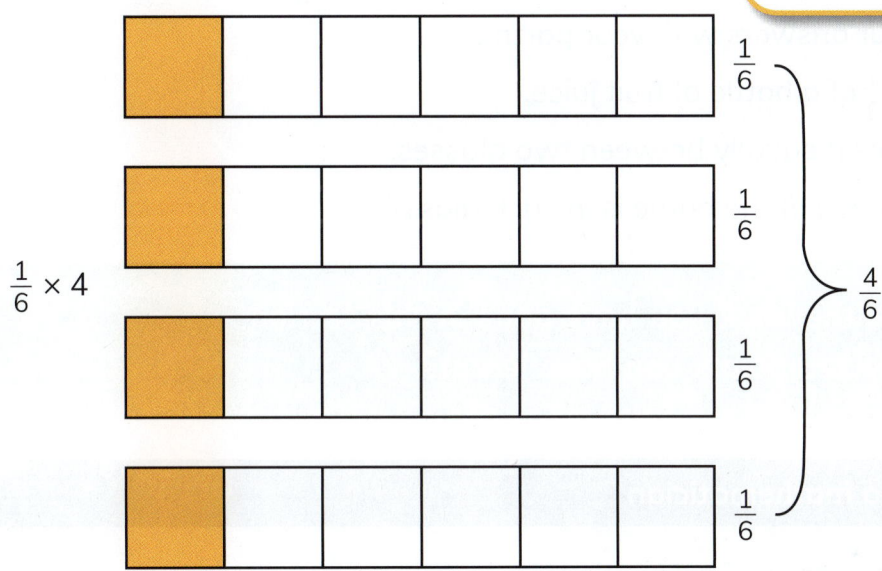

Kiki

$\frac{1}{6} \times 4 = \frac{4}{6}$

Magda

$\frac{1}{6} \times 4 = \frac{1}{6} + \frac{1}{6} + \frac{1}{6} + \frac{1}{6} = \frac{4}{6}$

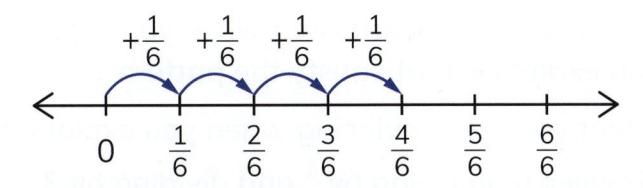

Which method do you prefer? Explain your answer.

Compare your answer with your partner.

Do you both prefer the same method?

15 Multiplying and dividing fractions and decimals

4 Draw a diagram to help you calculate $\frac{1}{3} \times 4$.

5 Arun multiplies a unit fraction by a whole number.

   He writes.

   $\frac{1}{5} \times 5 = \frac{5}{25}$

   Explain what Arun has done wrong.

6 Draw diagrams to help you calculate

   a $\frac{1}{5} \div 2$ b $\frac{1}{6} \div 3$ c $\frac{1}{4} \div 5$

   Check your answers with your partner.

7 Zara has $\frac{1}{3}$ of a bottle of fruit juice.

   She divides it equally between two glasses.

   What fraction of the bottle is in each glass?

> Look back at the work you have done in this section.
> What are the key points you have learnt?

Think like a mathematician

Look at these pairs of calculations.

$\frac{1}{2} \times 7 = \frac{7}{2}$ $7 \div 2 = \frac{7}{2}$

$\frac{1}{2} \times 6 = \frac{6}{2}$ $6 \div 2 = \frac{6}{2}$

$\frac{1}{2} \times 5 = \frac{5}{2}$ $5 \div 2 = \frac{5}{2}$

Write the next three rows of the pattern.

What do you notice about multiplying by $\frac{1}{2}$ and dividing by 2?

What happens if you multiply by $\frac{1}{3}$ and divide by 3?

- You will show that you are **generalising** when you explain the pattern and find examples that satisfy the pattern.

- You will show that you are **convincing** when you explain the relationship between multiplying by $\frac{1}{3}$ and dividing by 3.

15.2 Multiplying a decimal and a whole number

> **Look what I can do!**
> ☐ I can multiply a unit fraction by a whole number.
> ☐ I can divide a unit fraction by a whole number.

> 15.2 Multiplying a decimal and a whole number

We are going to ...
- multiply a number with 1 decimal place by a whole number.

Look at the picture.

> decimal   decimal place   decimal point

The girl is 90 cm tall.

The girl is twice as tall as the cat.

The cat is half or 0.5 times the height of the girl.

Half of 90 cm = 45 cm

0.5 × 90 = 45 cm

The cat is 45 cm tall.

In this section you will learn to multiply numbers with 1 decimal place by whole numbers.

15 Multiplying and dividing fractions and decimals

> **Worked example 2**
>
> Calculate 12.9 × 6

Estimate:

10 × 6 = 60 and

20 × 6 = 120

So the answer is between 60 and 120.

12.9 × 6

129 ÷ 10   × 6

= 129 × 6 ÷ 10

= 774 ÷ 10

= 77.4

Answer:

12.9 × 6 = 77.4

Start by estimating the size of the answer.

Write 12.9 as 129 ÷ 10

You can change the order of the multiplying and dividing.
(This uses the associative law.)

Multiply 129 by 6 and divide the answer by 10.

Check the answer against your estimate.

Exercise 15.2

1. Sofia counts in steps of zero-point-three.

   She says, 'zero-point-three, zero-point-six, ...'

   She continues counting to find 4 × 0.3.

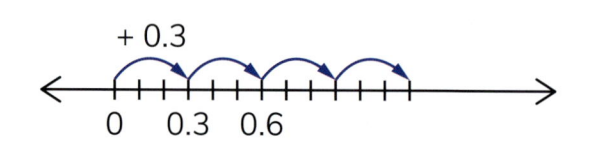

   What is her answer?

2. Draw a number line to help you calculate.

   a 7 × 0.4   b 5 × 0.5   c 3 × 0.9

3. A, B and C stand for missing numbers on this multiplication grid. Find the value of A, B and C.

×	6	5	A
0.5	B	2.5	2
0.2	1.2	C	0.8
0.6	3.6	3	2.4

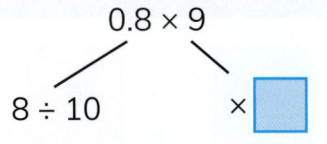

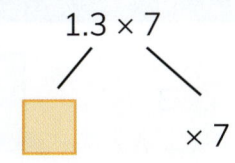

15.2 Multiplying a decimal and a whole number

4   Copy and complete these calculations.

a)   0.8 × 9
     ↙   ↘
   8 ÷ 10   × □

   = 8 × □ ÷ 10

   = □ ÷ 10

   = □

b)   1.3 × 7
     ↙   ↘
    □   × 7

   = 13 × 7 ÷ □

   = 91 ÷ □

   = □

> **Tip**
>
> Estimate your answer before you calculate it. You can use diagrams similar to those in question 4 to help you.

5   Calculate.

   a   0.6 × 7   b   1.4 × 5

6   Which calculation is the odd one out? Explain why.

   1.4 × 5   3.5 × 7   2.5 × 8   1.8 × 5   3.5 × 6

   Check your answers with your partner.
   Did you remember to estimate before you calculated the answer?

7   What is the product of 15.4 and 7?

8   Copy and complete these calculations.

a)
	1 •	6
×		7

b)
	7 •	3
×		4

c)
	2	6 •	2
×			5

> Look back over the methods you have used to multiply a decimal number by a whole number. Which method do you prefer? Why?

15 Multiplying and dividing fractions and decimals

Think like a mathematician

You need these cards.

| 3 | 5 | 4 | 6 |

Arrange the cards as a multiplication calculation.

Investigate different answers. Which one is the biggest? Which one is the smallest?
How many different answers can you find?

You will show you are **specialising** when you find solutions to the problem.

Look what I can do!

☐ I can multiply a number with 1 decimal place by a whole number.

Check your progress

Use any method you like to do these questions.
You can draw number lines or diagrams to help you.

1 Calculate.

   a $\frac{1}{6} \times 5$ b $9 \times \frac{1}{4}$ c $\frac{1}{7} \times 7$

2 Calculate.

   a $\frac{1}{6} \div 3$ b $\frac{1}{8} \div 7$ c $\frac{1}{5} \div 6$

3 Calculate.

   a 3.7×3 b 2.8×5 c 52.1×9

4 Arun is thinking of a unit fraction.

   He says, 'When I multiply my fraction by 5 it will be equivalent to $\frac{1}{2}$ and when I multiply it by 10 it is equivalent to 1.'

   What fraction is Arun thinking of?

5 Copy and complete this multiplication grid.

×	7	9	4
0.5			
0.6			
0.2			

16 Time

Getting started

1 Copy and complete these sentences.
   a There are _____ seconds in a minute.
   b There are _____ minutes in an hour.
   c There are _____ hours in a day.
   d There are _____ months in a year.
   e The month of April has _____ days.
   f The month of July has _____ days.

2 a Arun's favourite film is 2 hours and 15 minutes long.
      How long is the film in minutes?
   b Sofia's favourite film is 95 minutes long.
      How long is the film in hours and minutes?

3 This is Paulo's timetable for school on Mondays.

09:00	09:45	10:30	10:55	12:00	13:15	13:50	14:45	15:50
History	Maths	Break time	Music	Lunch time	Art	Science	Sports	School finishes

   a Write the time that Paulo's science lesson starts as a 12-hour clock time.
   b How long is Paulo's break time?
   c It takes Paulo 10 minutes to walk home after school. What time does he get home?

16 Time

Understanding, reading and calculating time are skills you will find useful in everyday life.

Fred and Yuri are talking to each other on the telephone.
It is daytime where Fred is, but where Yuri is it is night-time.

Can you explain why?
What do you know about different times around the world?

> 16.1 Time intervals and time zones

We are going to ...

- explore time intervals that are less than one second
- calculate time intervals
- compare times between different time zones.

Time and time intervals are used in lots of places every day. Trains and buses often follow a timetable so we can calculate the length of a journey or work out how long we will wait at a station.

time interval   time zone
Universal Time (UT)

16.1 Time intervals and time zones

When we want to contact people all over the world through the internet or by using the telephone, we can check the time difference to see if they will be awake.

Standard time around the world is based on Universal Time (UT) measured at Greenwich, England. Each 15° of longitude away from Greenwich is equal to 1 hour time difference. Times do often vary from this and follow along the borders of countries.

The Meridian Line in Greenwich

> **Worked example 1**
>
> Sara is going to a concert.
>
> The time is 5.37 p.m. and the concert starts at 7.15 p.m.
>
> How long does she have to wait for the concert to start?

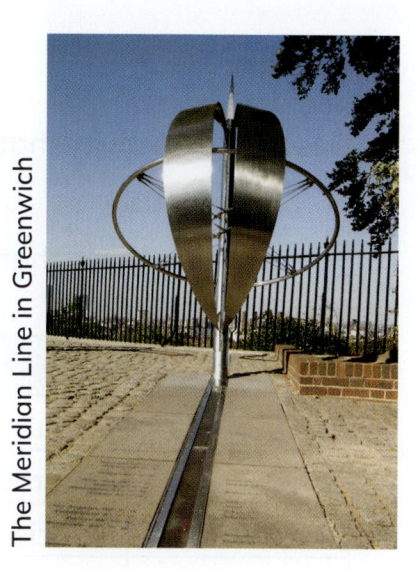

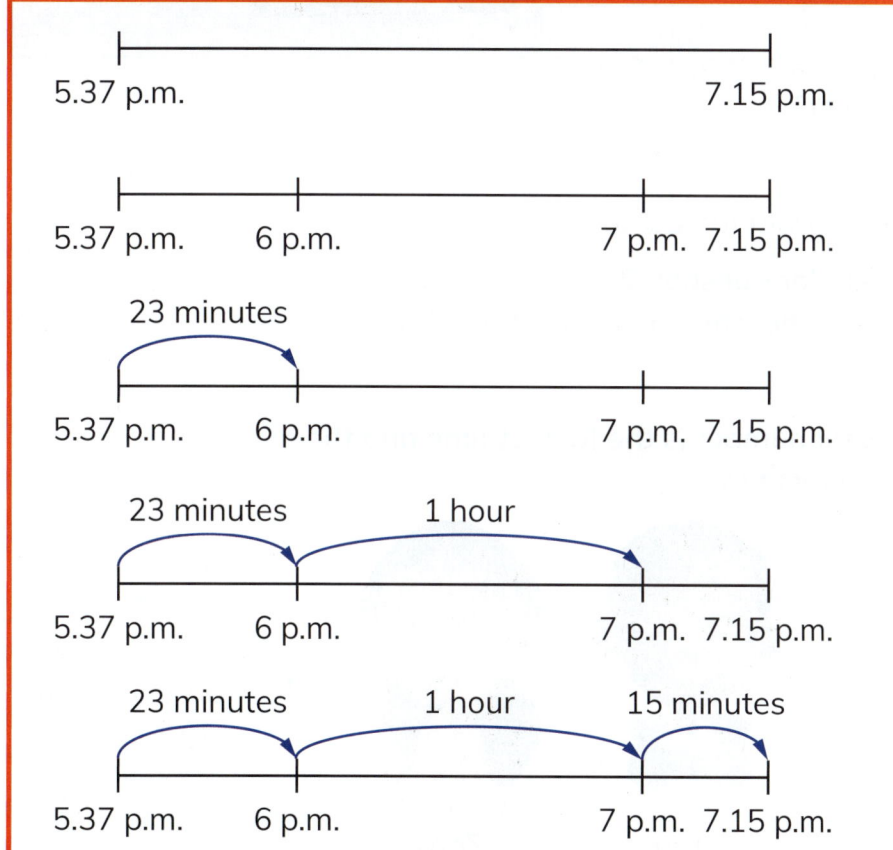

Timeline	Instruction
5.37 p.m. ————————————— 7.15 p.m.	Draw a time line and label the ends with the times 5.37 p.m. and 7.15 p.m.
5.37 p.m. — 6 p.m. ——— 7 p.m. — 7.15 p.m.	Label any whole hours between the two times.
23 minutes from 5.37 p.m. to 6 p.m.	Work out how many minutes there are between the first time and the first whole hour time.
23 minutes + 1 hour (6 p.m. to 7 p.m.)	Work out how many hours there are between the whole hour times.
23 minutes + 1 hour + 15 minutes	Work out how many minutes there are from the last whole hour time to the last time. Find the total time.

23 minutes + 1 hour + 15 minutes
= 1 hour and 38 minutes.

Answer:

Sara has to wait 1 hour and 38 minutes for the concert to start.

177

16 Time

Exercise 16.1

1. Describe an activity that takes approximately:

   a 0.5 seconds   b 5 seconds   c 0.5 minutes   d 5 minutes

2. These are the times that six motorbike riders took to travel around a race track.

Bike number	Rider's name	Time (seconds)
1	Markus	52.6
2	Eduardo	51.5
3	Francis	53.4
4	Daniel	53.1
5	Leke	52.3
6	Amir	52.9

   a Which rider was the fastest?

   b Which rider was the slowest?

   c Write all the times in order from fastest to slowest.

   Check your partner's answers for question 2.
   Talk to your partner about whether their answers show that they:

   - can compare two times
   - understand that the lowest number is the fastest time and the highest number is the slowest time.

3.
   Arun: I balanced on one leg for 2 minutes and 23 seconds.

   Zara: I balanced on one leg for 132 seconds.

   a Who balanced on one leg the longest?

   b Work with a partner to time how long you can balance on one leg. Write the time using minutes and seconds and write it again using only seconds.

16.1 Time intervals and time zones

4 Copy and complete the tables.

a
Number of days	0.5	1	1.5	2	2.5	3
Number of hours		24				

b
Number of hours	0.5	1	1.5	2	2.5	3
Number of minutes				120		

c
Number of minutes	0.5	1	1.5	2	2.5	3
Number of seconds			90			

Use this timetable to answer questions 5 to 8.

Train timetable			
	A	B	C
Ourtown	10:11	12:32	14:23
Riverton	10:47	13:08	14:59
Hillbury	11:17	13:38	15:29
Newcity	12:32	14:53	16:44

5 How long does it take for the train to travel:

   a from Ourtown to Riverton?   b from Hillbury to Newcity?

   c from Ourtown to Hillbury?   d from Ourtown to Newcity?

6 How long do I have to wait for a train if I arrive at:

   a Ourtown station at 09:42?   b Riverton station at 10:58?

   c Hillbury station at 13:17?   d Riverton station at 14:36?

7 Which is the latest train I can catch from Ourtown to arrive at:

   a Riverton station by 12:00?   b Hillbury station by 14:15?

   c Newcity station by 15:30?   d Hillbury station by 15:40?

8 Tara takes train C to Newcity. She arrives at Newcity station then walks home for 20 minutes. At what time does she arrive home?

16 Time

The world is divided into 24 time zones. This is a simple map showing approximate time zones. It shows how far ahead or behind the time is in hours from the Universal Time at '0'.

Many land time zone lines are moved to give countries a manageable time system. Some countries cross more than one time zone. Use this map to answer questions 9 to 11.

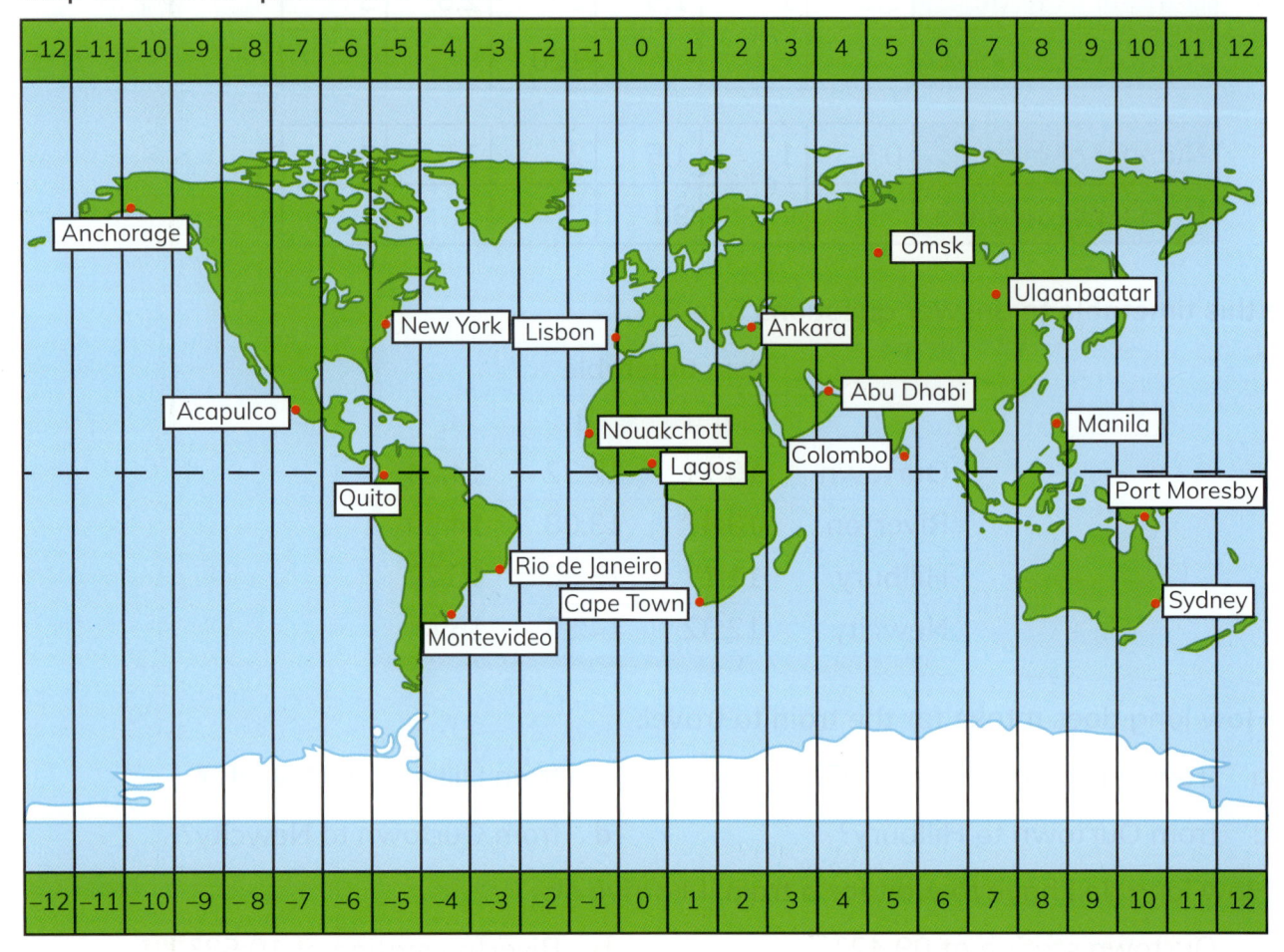

> **Tip**
>
> The map appears to show 25 time zones, but the 12 and −12 locations are the same. The world is a sphere so you need to imagine the map wrapping around so that two ends overlap.

9   What is the approximate time difference in hours between:

   a   Quito and Lagos?
   b   Anchorage and Colombo?
   c   Cape Town and Ulaanbaatar?
   d   Nouakchott and Sydney?

16.1 Time intervals and time zones

10 Use the map to estimate.

    a   If it was 09:21 in Lagos, what would be the time in Omsk?

    b   If it was 01:44 in Acapulco, what would be the time in Port Moresby?

    c   If it was 18:03 in Rio de Janeiro, what would be the time in Ankara?

    d   If it was 20:18 in Manila, what would be the time in Colombo?

11 If it was midday in Abu Dhabi, which place(s) on the map would have a different date to the date in Abu Dhabi?

Think like a mathematician

Sofia, Zara, Arun, and Marcus have all answered this question:

Amy called Eva on the telephone at 18:35 in Amy's country.
Eva's time zone is 5 hours ahead (+5) of Amy's time zone.
They spoke on the telephone for 48 minutes.
What was the time for Eva when the call finished?

These are their answers:

- Sofia: 14:23
- Zara: 19:23
- Arun: 23:83
- Marcus: 00:23

Which answer is correct?

Look carefully at the incorrect answers. Talk to your partner or group about what mistakes each person might have made in their working to reach the different answers.

Write down feedback to each child who got the question incorrect. Explain where they went wrong and how they could get the answer right next time.

- You are **critiquing** when you think about the mistakes each child might have made.
- You are **convincing** when you explain where each child went wrong.
- You are **improving** when you suggest how each child could get the answer right next time.

16 Time

Look back over your answers in this unit where you have worked out a time interval or the time in different time zones. Have you made mistakes like the ones in the Think like a mathematician activity? How will you remember not to make those mistakes?

Look what I can do!

☐ I can understand time intervals that are less than one second.

☐ I can calculate time intervals.

☐ I can compare the time between time zones.

Check your progress

1.
> **Cinema film listings**
>
> The First Dawn ★★★★★
>
> Running time 123 minutes
>
> The Second Sunset ★★★★
>
> Running time 1 hour and 52 minutes

a How long is the film 'The First Dawn' in hours and minutes?

b How long is the film 'The Second Sunset' in minutes?

16.1 Time intervals and time zones

Continued

2 This is a timetable for one bus journey. The bus starts at stop A and travels to all the stops in order until it reaches stop G.

Bus stops						
A	B	C	D	E	F	G
07:22	08:10	08:47	10:15	11:45	13:08	15:21

a How long does it take to get from stop A to stop B?

b How long does it take to get from stop E to stop F?

c Which part of the journey between two stops takes 1.5 hours?

3 Here are clocks showing the correct time for three friends around the world. It is daytime for all three friends.

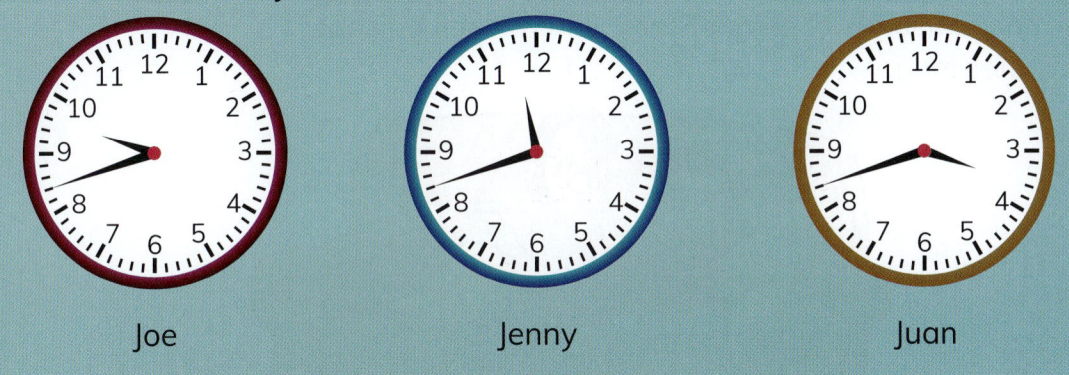

Joe   Jenny   Juan

a What is the time difference between where Joe is and where Juan is?

b What time will be showing on Jenny's clock in 1 hour and 30 minutes?

c Joe is expecting a phone call at 11 o'clock. How long does he have to wait?

Project 6 Time for bed

Project 6

Time for bed

Sarah and her younger brother, Harrison, are allowed to watch some television together before going to bed.

It is 6.15 p.m. now. Harrison's bedtime is 7.45 p.m. and Sarah's bedtime is 8.15 p.m.

They have a choice of watching:

- A film called 'Jungle Escape', which is 89 minutes long.
- One or more episodes of 'Duck and Goose', where each episode is 11 minutes long.
- One or more episodes of 'Swim Stars', where each episode is 23 minutes long.

1 What could Sarah watch after Harrison has gone to bed, assuming that she doesn't want to leave part of a programme unwatched?

2 What could they watch together before Harrison has to go to bed, assuming that Harrison does not want to go upstairs part-way through a programme?

Can you find another different combination of programmes they could watch together?

Can you find *all* the different combinations of programmes they could watch together?

How do you know you have found them all?

17 Number and the laws of arithmetic

> **Getting started**
>
> 1 Amy wrote these calculations.
>
>   Write true or false for each one.
>
>   a $108 + 6 = 6 + 108$ b $108 - 6 = 6 - 108$
>
>   c $108 \times 6 = 6 \times 108$ d $108 \div 6 = 6 \div 108$
>
> 2 Arun and Marcus calculate $19 \times 2 \times 5$
>
>   Arun   Marcus
>
> $19 \times 2 \times 5$ $19 \times 2 \times 5$
>
>   = ☐ × ☐   = ☐ × ☐
>
>   = ☐   = ☐
>
>   Copy and complete their calculations.
>
>   Which boy chose the better method?
>   Explain your answer.

The earliest recorded calculating device is the abacus.

Did you use an abacus when you started to learn about numbers?

The abacus on the next page shows a number pattern: $1 + 9 = 10$, $2 + 8 = 10$ and so on.

Gradually you learned these facts and were able to use them to help you work out other facts.

For example, if you know $2 + 8 = 10$, what other facts can you work out?

17 Number and the laws of arithmetic

Modern calculating devices include calculators and computers. These need to be programmed with rules so that they calculate correctly.

In this unit, you will learn about the rules of arithmetic and how they can be used to simplify calculations.

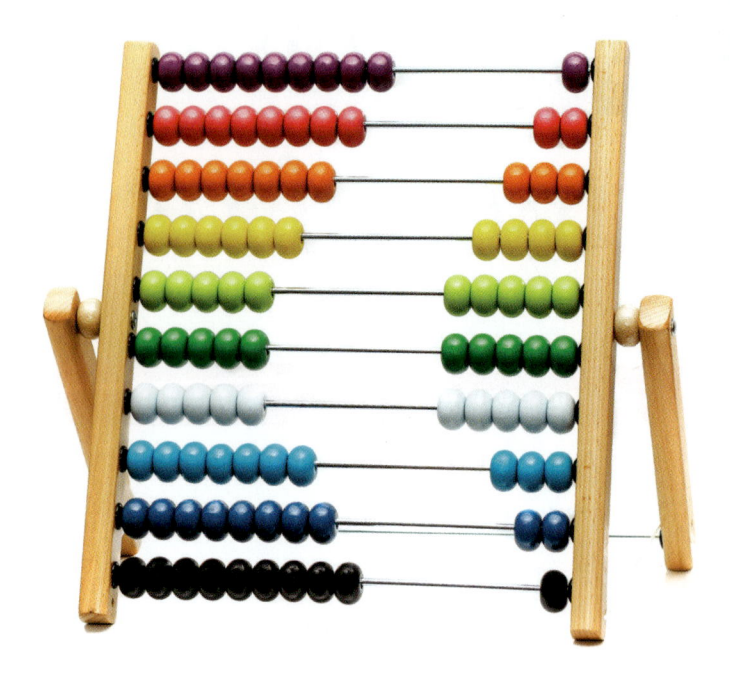

> 17.1 The laws of arithmetic

> **We are going to ...**
>
> - add and multiply numbers in different ways, using the associative law and the commutative law
> - break a multiplication fact into a sum of two other multiplication facts using the distributive law
> - carry out operations in a particular order: multiplication and division, then addition and subtraction.

Sometimes the best way to work out calculations is to use mental methods or pencil and paper jottings.

There are some rules that can make calculations easier.

For example, solve 7 + 38:

> associative law
> commutative law
> distributive law
> decompose
> regroup

> It is easier to start with 38 and then add on 7. I can use the commutative rule to write:
> 7 + 38 = 38 + 7 = 45

Can you think of any other rules to help you with calculations?

17 Number and the laws of arithmetic

> **Worked example 1**
>
> Sofia writes $4 + 9 \times 5 = 65$.
>
> Is she correct?
>
> Explain your answer.

$4 + 9 \times 5$	Use the correct order of operations:
$= 4 + 45$	• multiplication and division
$= 49$	then
	• addition and subtraction.

Answer: No, Sofia is not correct.

She has not carried out the operations in the correct order.

She added first and then multiplied.

When you check Sofia's answer and work out why it is not correct, you are **critiquing**.

Exercise 17.1

1 Use the digits 2, 5, 6 and 7 once each time to complete this calculation in four different ways.

$$\square \times \square \times \square \times \square = $$

Work out the answer to each calculation.

What do you notice?

Check your results with your partner.

2 Sofia wrote these statements.

Write true or false for each one. Explain those that are false.

  a $88 + 16 = 66 + 88$

  b $18 \div 6 = 6 \div 18$

  c $34 \times 16 = 16 \times 34$

  d $56 - 6 = 6 - 56$

17.1 The laws of arithmetic

3 Copy and complete these calculations.

a 17 × 2

☐ × 2 = 20   +   ☐ × 2 = ☐

= ☐

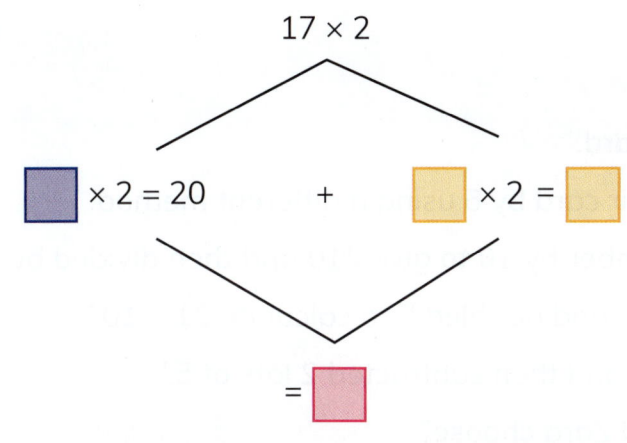

b 25 × 9 × 4 = 25 × ☐ × 9

= ☐ × 9

= ☐

4 Use the distributive law to help you work out these calculations. Show your working.

a 36 × 8   b 48 × 7   c 19 × 6

5 Use the associative law to help you work out these calculations. Show your working.

a 50 × 16 × 2   b 25 × 17 × 4   c 15 × 17 × 6

6 Calculate.

a 6 + 7 × 9   b 14 − 2 × 7   c 54 + 9 ÷ 3

7 Use +, −, × and ÷ to copy and complete these number sentences.

Example: 3 × 4 − 6 = 6

a 4 ☐ 6 ☐ 3 = 6   b 5 ☐ 6 ☐ 2 = 28
c 5 ☐ 9 ☐ 3 = 8   d 8 ☐ 2 ☐ 4 = 0

8 Here are five multiplication calculations.

54 × 6   22 × 3   41 × 5   19 × 4   37 × 6

Show how you would do each calculation.

Explain your methods to your partner.

Did you make the same decisions?

17 Number and the laws of arithmetic

9 Here are three number cards.

   [42] [21] [38]

   Sofia, Arun and Zara each choose a card.

   They each multiply the number on their card by 5 using a different method.

   • Sofia says, 'I multiplied my number by 10 to give 210 and then divided by 2.'
   • Arun says, 'I halved my number and doubled 5 to calculate 21 × 10.'
   • Zara says, 'I multiplied 40 by 5 and then subtracted 2 lots of 5.'

   a Which number did Sofia, Arun and Zara choose?
   b Which of these methods of multiplying by 5 would you choose? Explain your decision.

Look back at the questions and your answers.
Think about how you can improve your work.

Think like a mathematician

Numbers and operations

Write down two different 2-digit numbers:

- multiply one of the numbers by 5
- add 36
- multiply by 20
- add the other 2-digit number
- subtract 720.

Choose different starting numbers. What happens?
Does it always work for any starting number?

You will show you are **generalising** and **convincing** when you notice and explain what happens.

17.1 The laws of arithmetic

Look what I can do!

☐ I can add and multiply numbers in different ways, using the associative law and the commutative law.

☐ I can break a multiplication fact into a sum of two other multiplication facts using the distributive law.

☐ I can do operations in a particular order: multiplication and division, then addition and subtraction.

Check your progress

1. Arun calculates 6 × 5 × 9 × 2 mentally.

   He says, 'I can find the answer by multiplying 54 by 10.'

   Explain how he knows this.

2. Marcus calculates 19 × 4 using this method:

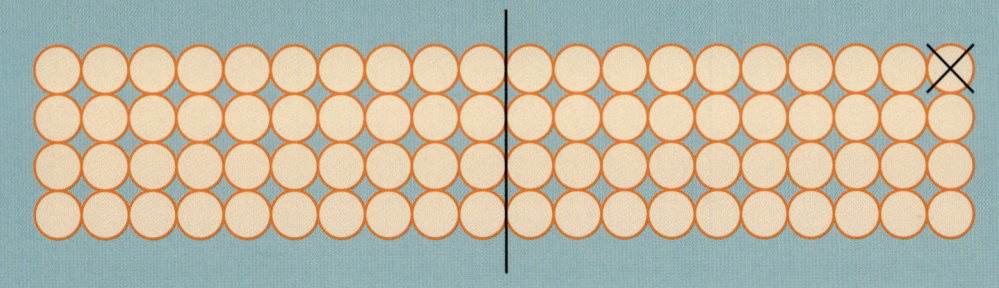

   20 × 4 = 80
   80 − 1 = 79

   Explain Marcus's mistake.

3. Calculate.

   a   16 + 8 ÷ 4   b   16 − 3 × 2   c   8 × 7 − 2

4. Copy and complete this calculation.

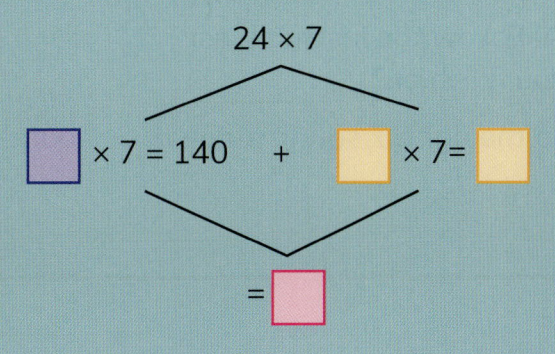

   24 × 7

   ☐ × 7 = 140   +   ☐ × 7 = ☐

   = ☐

18 > Position and direction

> **Getting started**
>
> 1   What are the coordinates of the points A to E?
>
> (Grid showing points: A at (0,1), B at (2,6), C at (3,0), D at (4,4), E at (6,5))
>
> 2   Draw a coordinate grid.
>
>   Label the x-axis and the y-axis.
>
>   Number the x-axis from 0 to 5. Number the y-axis from 0 to 5.
>
>   Mark these coordinates on the grid.
>
>   A   (1, 4)   B   (0, 5)   C   (3, 2)   D   (0, 0)   E   (4, 0)
>
> 3   Start on square A. Follow the instructions.
>   Which letter do you finish on?
>
>   Move 3 squares to the right, 2 squares down, 1 square left,
>   1 square up.
>
> | A | B | C | D |
> |---|---|---|---|
> | E | F | G | H |
> | I | J | K | L |
> | M | N | O | P |

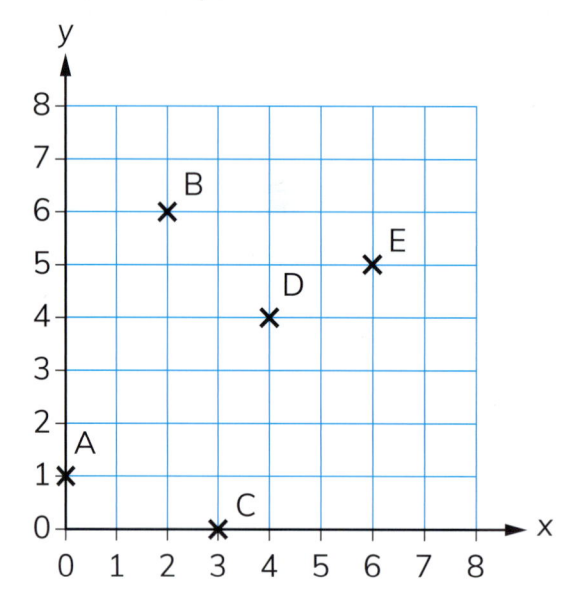

192 >

18 Position and direction

Coordinates make it possible for us to communicate about the position of places and objects.

A playground is going to be built on the land on this map.
It must not be close to the wall or the trees.

Where on the land would you recommend building the playground?
Give the coordinates of possible places. Why would you build it there?

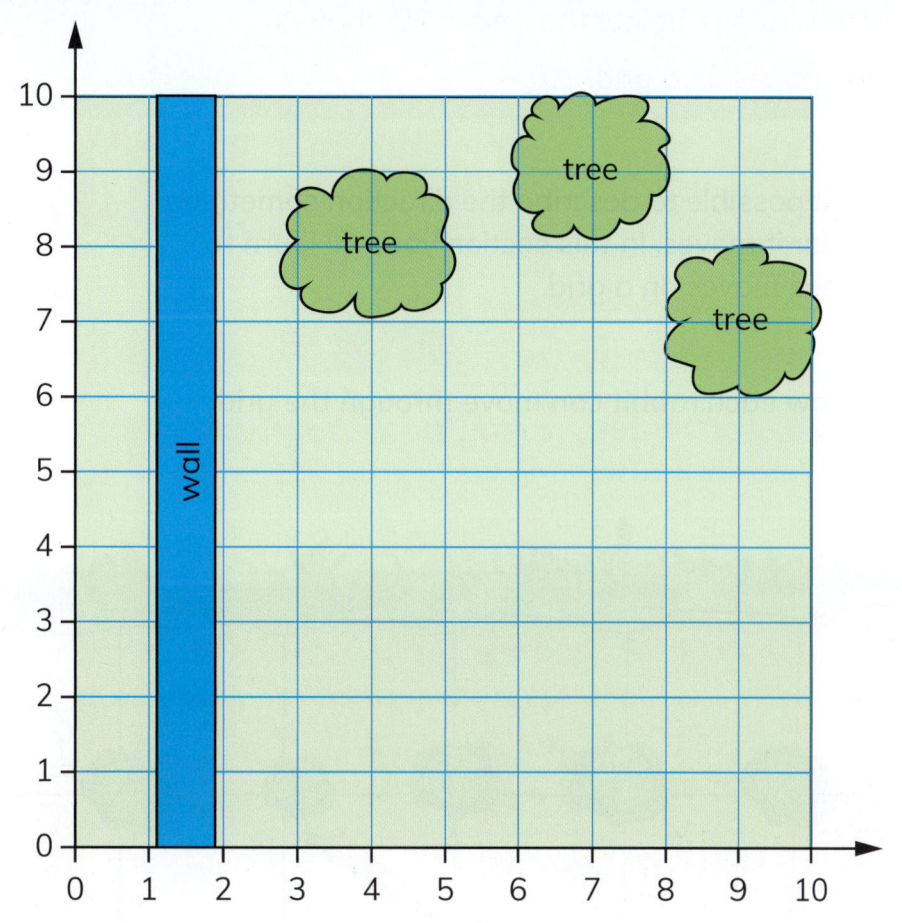

18 Position and direction

> 18.1 Coordinates and translation

We are going to …
- use coordinates to compare positions
- use coordinates to plot points that make 2D shapes
- translate 2D shapes on a grid.

Translation makes it possible to describe the direction something moves in and how far it moves. In this section you will learn to describe how a shape moves on a grid.

coordinates
translation

Look at this grid.

Can you describe how each rabbit can move through the grid to get to the carrot?

18.1 Coordinates and translation

> **Worked example 1**

Describe the translation of the shaded shape to the unshaded shape.

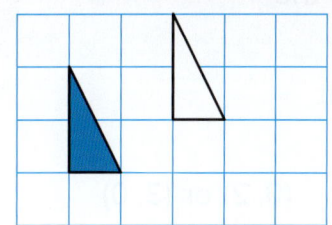

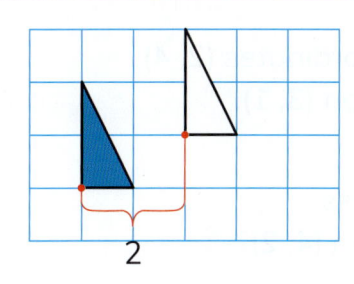

Choose one vertex of the original shape.

Count how many squares horizontally (left or right) the vertex moves to its position on the translated shape.

This shape has been translated 2 squares to the right.

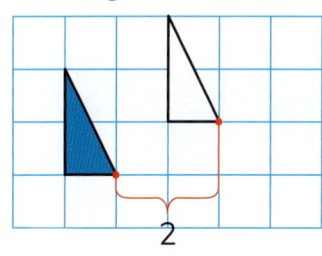

Check using another vertex.

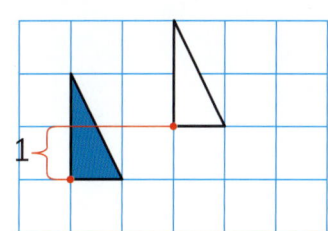

Choose one vertex of the original shape.

Count how many squares vertically (up or down) the vertex has moved to the position of the translated shape.

This shape has been translated 1 square up.

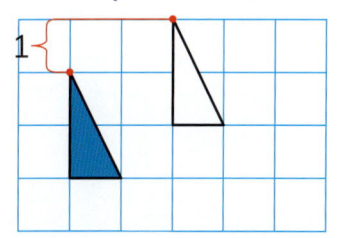

Check using another vertex.

Answer:
The shape has been translated 2 squares to the right and 1 square up.

195

18 Position and direction

Exercise 18.1

1. Draw a coordinate grid on squared paper with the x-axis and the y-axis labelled from 0 to 5.

   For each pair of coordinates, write the coordinates of the point that is closer to (0, 0).

   a (3, 0) or (5, 0)   b (0, 2) or (0, 4)   c (0, 2) or (3, 0)
   d (4, 1) or (3, 5)   e (2, 3) or (3, 1)

2. On the coordinate grid, there is a tree at the position with coordinates (2, 4). Sarah is standing at the position (1, 3). Pasha is at the position (3, 1). Who is closer to the tree?

3. The numbers are not labelled on this coordinate grid. The cross marks the position (3, 5). Which letter is closest to the position (4, 2)?

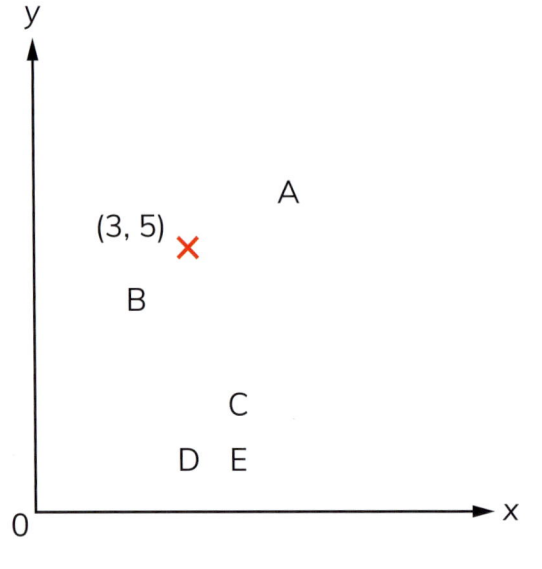

4. a Estimate the coordinates for the position of letter Z.

   b Write down what you would say to convince your partner that your estimate is correct.

   c Discuss your answer with your partner. How could you or your partner improve your estimates? Alternatively, how could you make your argument more convincing?

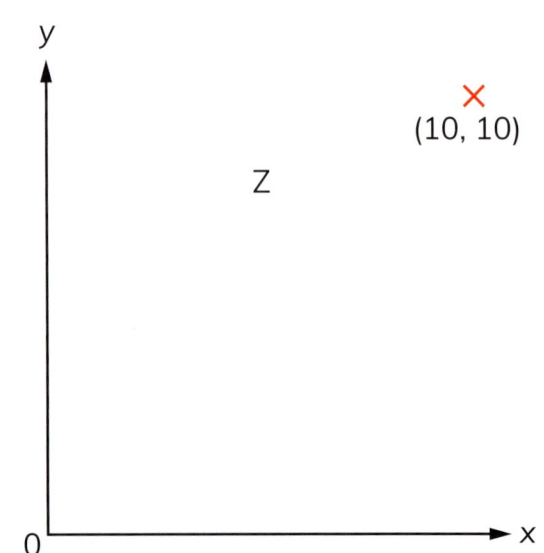

18.1 Coordinates and translation

5 (1, 3), (1, 2) and (4, 2) are the coordinates of three vertices of a rectangle. Plot these on a grid. What are the coordinates of the other vertex?

6 (2, 4) and (4, 2) are the coordinates of two vertices of a square. Plot these on a grid. What could the other vertices of the square be? Find all the possible solutions.

> There are three possible solutions to question 6. Have you found them all? Think about which solutions you found quickly and which took more time. How can you remember to look for different solutions in the future?

7 Look at the shapes on this grid.

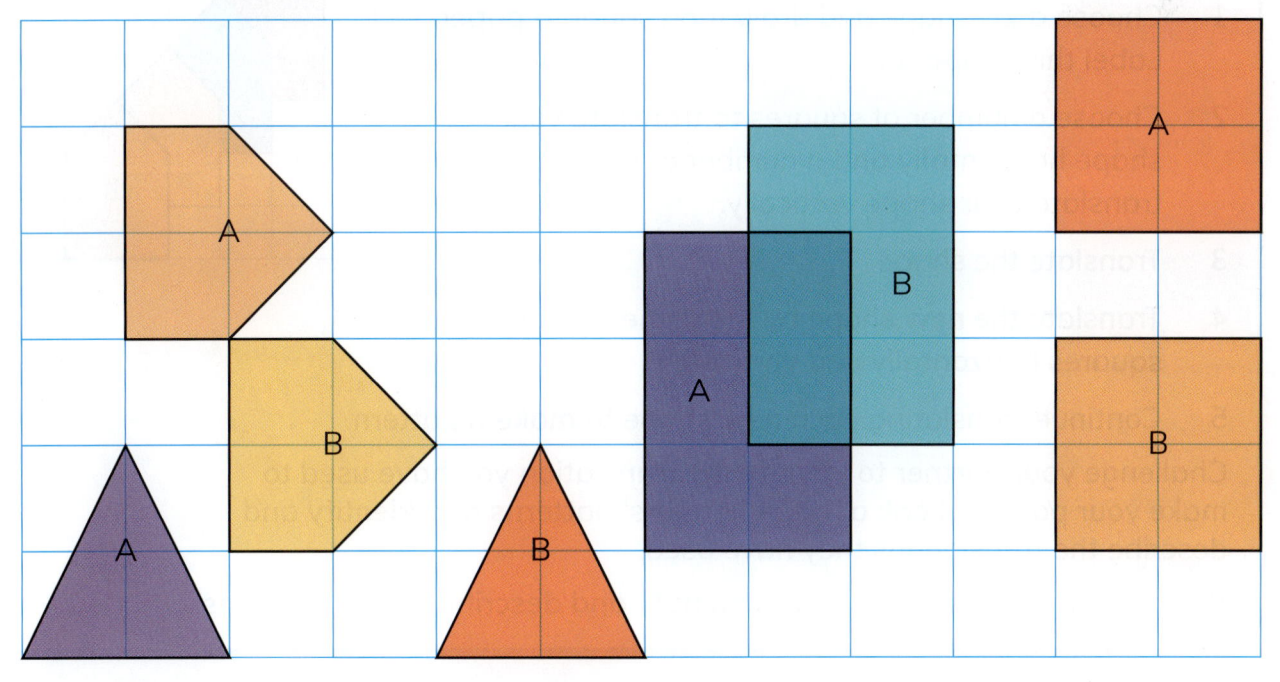

Name the shape that has been translated and how its colour has changed. For example, you could write 'orange square B to red square A'.

a 4 squares to the right
b 3 squares down
c 1 square left and 2 squares up
d 1 square right and 1 square up

18 Position and direction

8   Copy this shape onto squared paper.
    Translate the shape 3 squares to the right and 2 squares down.

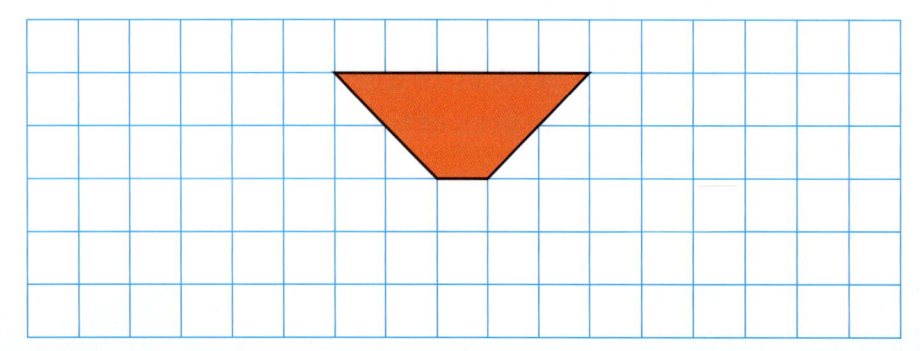

> **Think like a mathematician**
>
> Make a pattern like this using translation.
>
> 1   Choose a 2D shape and draw it on squared paper. Label this shape '1'.
> 2   Choose a number of squares to translate your shape horizontally and a number of squares to translate your shape vertically.
> 3   Translate the shape.
> 4   Translate the new shape by the same number of squares horizontally and vertically.
> 5   Continue translating each new shape to make a pattern.
>
> Challenge your partner to identify the translation you have used to make your pattern. Look at other learners' patterns and identify and describe the translations they have used.
>
> You are **characterising** when you identify and describe the translations.

Look what I can do!

☐   I can use coordinates to compare positions.

☐   I can use coordinates to plot points that make 2D shapes.

☐   I can translate 2D shapes on a grid.

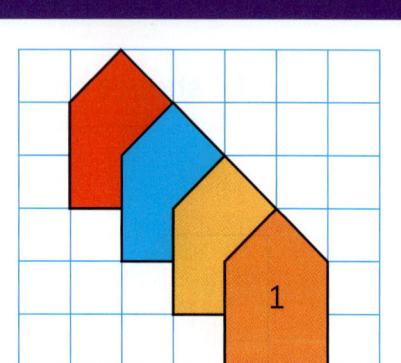

18.1 Coordinates and translation

Check your progress

1. There is a tree at the point (5, 2).
   What are the coordinates of the flower that is closest to the tree?

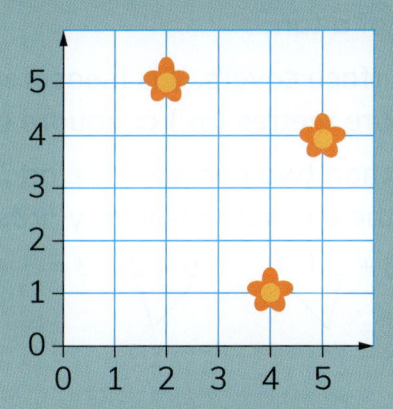

2. Write these coordinates in order of their distance from the y-axis.
   Start with the coordinate closest to the y-axis.

   (4, 0)   (2, 1)   (3, 3)   (0, 5)

3. (3, 4), (3, 7) and (6, 7) are the coordinates of three vertices of a square.
   What are the coordinates of the other vertex?

4. Describe the translation of shape A to shape B.

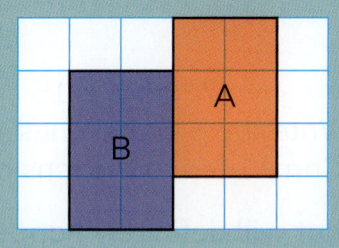

5. Copy this shape on squared paper.
   Translate the shape 3 squares to the right and 2 squares up.

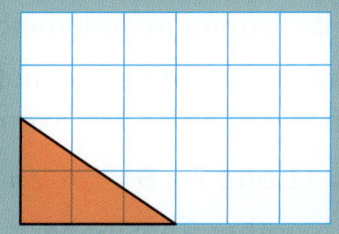

Glossary

angle	the amount of a turn	24
area	the size a surface covers. It is measured in square units, such as square metres (m²) or square centimetres (cm²).	154
associative law	when more than two numbers are added or multiplied, you can do the calculations in any order. For example:	

$$8 + 3 + 4 = 8 + 3 + 4 \qquad 5 \times 2 \times 3 = 5 \times 2 \times 3$$
$$11 + 4 = 8 + 7 \qquad\qquad 10 \times 3 = 5 \times 6$$
$$15 = 15 \qquad\qquad\qquad 30 = 30 \qquad\qquad 172$$

average	a way to describe a set of data. It could be the most usual value or the middle value in a set of data.	15
bar chart	a graph with information organised into bars. The length of a bar shows the frequency it represents.	96
carry, carrying	lift a number and take it to another place. For example:	

```
   4 8
 + 4 7
 -----
   9 5
   1
```
   7 add 8 is 15
   Write the 5 in the 'ones' column
   Carry 1 ten to the tens column   60

certain	an outcome that will definitely happen	88
common denominator	a common multiple of the denominators of two or more fractions. For example, 9 is a common denominator for $\frac{1}{3}$ and $\frac{1}{9}$ and 12 is a common denominator for $\frac{1}{3}$ and $\frac{1}{4}$.	104
commutative law	when two numbers are added or multiplied, you can do the calculation in any order. For example: $7 + 4 = 4 + 7 = 11$ and $7 \times 5 = 5 \times 7 = 35$	187
compose	put a number together from its parts (hundreds, tens and ones), for example $600 + 30 + 2 = 632$	12
composite number	a number with more than two factors. For example, 6 has the factors 1, 2, 3 and 6.	36

coordinates	a pair of numbers that gives a position on a grid. The first number gives the horizontal position. The second number gives the vertical position.	192
cube	a 3D shape with exactly 6 square faces	68
data	a collection of information	50
decimal number	a number written in decimal notation, for example, 34.5	11
decimal place	the number of digits to the right of the decimal point: for example, the number 45.67 has two decimal places	15

decimal point — the decimal point separates whole numbers from decimal places:

10s	1s	$\frac{1}{10}$s	$\frac{1}{100}$s
5	7	0	8

You read 57.08 as 'fifty-seven point zero eight'.   12

decompose	break down a number into its parts (hundreds, tens and ones), for example, 456 is 400 + 50 + 6	10
degree	a unit of measurement for angles	108
°	the symbol used for degrees	112
denominator	the bottom number of a fraction. It tells you how many equal parts a shape or quantity has been divided into.	76
distributive law	when two numbers are multiplied, you can break one number into two parts and keep the second number the same, then work with two simpler multiplications. Add the products to give the answer.	

$$16 \times 4$$
(Break 16 into 10 + 6)

$10 \times 4 = 40$ + $6 \times 4 = 24$ (Work with two multiplications)

= 64   (Find the sum of the two multiplications)   187

divisible	can be divided without a remainder. For example, 14 is divisible by 2.	116

divisibility test	a test for finding whether one whole number is divisible by another. For example, a number can be divided by .... • 4 if the number made by the last two digits (tens and ones) is divisible by 4 • 8 if the number made by the last three digits (hundreds, tens and ones) is divisible by 8.	124
divisor	a number by which another number is divided, for example: 30 ÷ 3 = 10 ↑ divisor	121
dot plot	a graph with information represented by dots. The height of the dot shows the frequency it represents.	130
equally likely	outcomes have the same chance of happening	89
equilateral triangle	a triangle with three equal sides and three equal angles; a regular triangle	24
even chance	there is the same chance that an outcome will happen or will not happen	88
factor	a whole number that divides exactly into another number. For example, 6 divides exactly by 2 and 3 so 2 and 3 are factors of 6.	43
frequency diagram	a graph with information organised into bars which represent the frequencies of ranges or intervals. Frequency diagrams are used for continuous data, such as measures. There are no gaps between bars in a frequency diagram.	137
hundredth	one of one hundred equal parts. As a decimal it is written as 0.01.	12
impossible	there is no chance that an outcome will happen	90
improper fraction	a fraction where the numerator is greater than or equal to the denominator. For example, $\frac{5}{3}$ (five thirds).	83
integer	a positive or negative number or zero but not a decimal or fraction	64
inverse operations	operations that are the opposite of each other. For example, the inverse of add 2 is subtract 2 the inverse of multiply by 5 is divide by 5 +2 ×5 10 12 7 35 −2 ÷5	121

isosceles triangle	a triangle with exactly two equal sides and two equal angles	24
likely	there is a high chance that an outcome will happen	89
line graph	a graph that uses one or more lines to join points which represent a data set	137
line of symmetry	the line that could be drawn on a shape or pattern so that the shape or pattern on one side of the line exactly mirrors the other side of the line	28
linear sequence	a number pattern which increases or decreases by the same amount each time; for example, the pattern 2, 6, 10, 14, … follows the rule 'add 4'	36
median	a type of average which is the middle value after the data has been arranged in order	50
mixed number	a whole number and a proper fraction combined. For example, $1\frac{3}{4}$.	83
mode	a type of average which is the value that occurs the most in a set of data	50
multiple	the result of multiplying a number by a positive whole number. For example, the first few multiples of 3 are: 3, 6, 9, 12, …	35
nearest	closest	15
negative number	a number that is less than zero. We use a – sign to show a negative number. ←−−−−−−−−−−−−−−−−−−−−−−−→ −10 0 10 negative numbers	positive numbers	37
numerator	the top number of a fraction. It tells you how many parts you have.	76
open cube	a shape made with exactly 5 square faces; a cube with one face missing	68
operator	a fraction used to find a part of an amount. For example, to find $\frac{3}{4}$ of something, you either divide by 4 and then multiply by 3 or multiply by 3 and then divide by 4.	76

outcome	the result of an event in a probability experiment	90
per cent	the number of parts in a hundred	79
percentage	the number of parts out of a hundred. The symbol is %.	58
perimeter	the total distance around the outside of a shape. It is measured in units of length, such as metres (m) or centimetres (cm).	154
place value	the value of a digit determined by its position. For example, in 830 the 3 has a value of 3 tens (30).	11

100s	10s	1s
8	3	0

positive number	a number that is greater than zero

−10 ← negative numbers | 0 | positive numbers → 10 | 63 |
| prime number | a number with exactly two factors. For example: 2, 3, 5, 7, 11, ...

Remember: 1 is not a prime number. It has only one factor: 1. | 36 |
| product | the answer when two or more numbers are multiplied together. For example, the product of 3 and 5 is 15 because 3 × 5 = 15. | 116 |
| proper fraction | a fraction smaller than a whole. The numerator is smaller than the denominator, for example, $\frac{2}{5}$. | 76 |
| proportion | a portion or part of a whole. Proportion compares part to whole.

We say, '1 in every 4 squares is grey' or '1 out of every four squares is grey'. | 132 |

ratio	a comparison between two or more quantities. Ratio compares part to part.	
	We say, 'for every 1 grey square, there are 3 white squares'.	149
reflex angle	an angle that is greater than 180 degrees and less than 360 degrees	110
regroup	change the way a number is written. For example, you can write 456 as 400 + 50 + 6 or you can change it to 400 + 40 + 10 + 6.	57
repeated addition	a process of repeatedly adding the same number which can be used as a strategy for multiplication. For example, $\frac{1}{5} \times 4 = \frac{4}{5}$	168
round	change a number to a simpler value when an accurate answer is not needed	15
round to the nearest ...	you can round a number to the nearest whole number (10, 100 and so on). For example, 65.8 rounded to the nearest whole number is 66.	15
	65.8 is closer to 66 than to 65	
scalene triangle	a triangle with no equal sides and no equal angles	24

sequence	an ordered set of numbers, shapes or other mathematical objects arranged according to a rule. For example: 3, 6, 9, 12, 15, ... or ■ ● ▲ ■ ● ▲ ■ ...	35
simulation	a model of a real activity created to solve a problem	94
spatial pattern	a pattern that includes drawings. For example, these patterns form square numbers: 1, 4, 9, 16 or 1, 4, 9, 16	40
square number	a number you get when you multiply an integer by itself. For example, 16 is a square number. $4 \times 4 = 4^2 = 16$	36
statistical question	a question that can have different answers, so you need to collect data to be able to answer it	131
symbol	a thing that represents or stands for something else. For example, a ■, ● or ▲ could stand for a missing number.	59
symmetrical	a shape, pattern or picture with one side that exactly mirrors the other	27
tenth	one part in ten equal parts. As a decimal it is written as 0.1.	12
term	an item in a sequence. For example, in the sequence 4, 7, 10, 13, ... the second term is 7.	35

term-to-term rule	a rule you can use to find out how to get from one term to the next. For example, in the sequence 7, 10, 13, … the term-to-term rule is 'add 3'.	35
time interval	the amount of time that passes between two times	176
time zone	a region of the world that shares a common time	176
translation	to move a shape horizontally and/or vertically without rotating or flipping it	194
triangular number	triangular numbers can be shown as patterns of dots arranged as a triangle. Each row contains one extra dot. For example, 1, 3, 6, 10, …	36
unit fraction	a fraction with a numerator of 1, for example, $\frac{1}{2}$ or $\frac{1}{5}$	102
Universal Time (UT)	a time standard based on the time measured at Greenwich, England. It is also called Greenwich Mean Time (GMT).	177
unlikely	there is a low chance that an outcome will happen	90
Venn diagram	a diagram using hoops to sort items such as objects, shapes or numbers. It can show the relationship between up to three sets of items.	45
waffle diagram	a rectangular grid that represents proportions in data to show percentages and proportions of the whole sample or population	131

Acknowledgements

It takes a number of people to put together a new series of resources and their comments, support and encouragement have been really important to us.

From Mary Wood: With thanks to Katherine Bird, my editor, for her wise words, to my son, David, for his willingness to talk mathematics and respond to my IT needs and to my husband, Norman, for being there when it was tough going.

From Emma Low: With thanks to Katherine and Caroline for their indispensable ideas and feedback, and also to Andy and our daughters Natasha, Jessica and Phoebe for their love and support and occasional very helpful puzzle and problem testing.

From Cambridge University Press: We would like to thank the following people: Katherine Bird and Suzanne Thurston for their support for the authors; Lynne McClure for her feedback and comments on early sections of the manuscript; Thomas Carter, Caroline Walton, Laura Collins, Charlotte Griggs, Gabby Martin, Elizabeth Scurfield, Berenice Howard-Smith, Zohir Naciri, Emma McCrea and Eddie Rippeth as part of the team at Cambridge preparing the resources. We would also like to particularly thank all of the anonymous reviewers for their time and comments on the manuscript and as part of the endorsement process.

The authors and publishers acknowledge the following sources of copyright material and are grateful for the permissions granted. While every effort has been made, it has not always been possible to identify the sources of all the material used, or to trace all copyright holders. If any omissions are brought to our notice, we will be happy to include the appropriate acknowledgements on reprinting.

Thanks to the following for permission to reproduce images:

Cover illustration: Omar Aranda (Beehive Illustration)

JaysonPhotography/GI; Katie Fitch/EyeEm/GI; Ariel Skelley/GI; Buena Vista Images/GI; joSon/GI; Chaithanya Krishnan/GI; weifang/GI; Vibgyor78 - / 500px/GI; Norman Posselt/GI; Chris Griffiths/GI; Richard Drury/GI; EThamPhoto/GI; Kanchanalak Chanthaphun/EyeEm/GI; Peter Dazeley/GI; Mordolff/GI; Burazin/GI; Erik Witsoe/EyeEm/GI; Andy Andrews/GI; John M Lund Photography Inc/GI; Reinhard Krull/EyeEm/GI; SireAnko/GI; Peter Dazeley/GI; Peter Dazeley/GI; Priscila Zambotto/GI; JLGutierrez/GI; Catherine McQueen/GI; vpopovic/GI; Oleksiy Maksymenko/GI; Stephen Barnes/GI; R.Tsubin/GI; georgeclerk/GI; Thomas Winz/GI; askmenow/GI; Allexxandar/GI; blackred/GI; Lorado/GI; Dag Sundberg/GI; krisanapong detraphiphat/GI; David Malan/GI; Alex Roberts/EyeEm/GI; Brian Hagiwara/GI; Mohamad Faizal Ramli/EyeEm/GI; Kmatta/GI; Alistair Berg/GI; artpartner-images/GI; mattjeacock/GI; Aitor Diago/GI; MirageC/GI; Tahreer Photography/GI; Ning Li/GI; Steven Errico/GI; Photo by Bill Birtwhistle/GI; Germán Vogel/GI; aopsan/GI; Grant Faint/GI; Klaus Vedfelt/GI; Alex Segre/GI; Glowimages/GI; PM Images/GI; Ali Çobanoğlu/GI; Christian Horz/EyeEm/GI; Jamie Grill/GI; porcorex/GI; Chakrapong Worathat/EyeEm/GI

GI = Getty Images